DAKAR,
A WOLF'S ADVENTURE

By

Louis Dorfman

ISBN: 1-4107-3285-1 (e-book)
ISBN: 1-4107-3286-X (Paperback)
ISBN: 1-4107-3287-8 (Dust Jacket)

Library of Congress Control Number: 2003092089

This book is printed on acid free paper.

Printed in the United States of America
Bloomington, IN

1stBooks – rev. 03/31/03

CHAPTER 1

In the cool gray mist of the early Canadian morning, nine objects floated out of the heavy forest of western redcedar and western hemlock. They blended into the surrounding scenery so well; a human would only be able to recognize their presence by their movement. They moved silently through the melting snow of early spring. Their colors were that of the winter landscape: grey, black, and white blending together in a pattern that was perfectly suited to their surroundings.

Dakar, one of the three cubs in the pack, looked at his mother, Tanya. How grand she was! He was so proud of the way all the pack members looked up to her. She was the female leader of the pack, the counterpart to Torga, her mate. By pack tradition, she was the only female allowed to have cubs. Dakar was only eleven months old, and he never ventured far from his mother's side. He only felt safe when he could see his mother. She was almost snow-white, and her dignified attitude made all the rest of the pack respect her completely. While the other adult wolves loved to play games with each other and occasionally act like little cubs themselves, Tanya never lost her

1

noble bearing, and she would simply smile tolerantly and stand to the side when the others began their play.

Dakar thought that there could not be a more wonderful mother in the world than his beloved Tanya. Three months earlier Dakar's sister, Miya, had died in a fierce winter storm; it swept over the entire northern range of the Rocky Mountains that the pack called home. Tanya had taken particular care to protect Miya; she had always been the frailest of the cubs. During the harsh winter Tanya had gone without sleep many nights to watch over Miya and make sure she had plenty of milk. When Miya died, Tanya had almost lost her composure. She howled for three days, almost constantly. Then, however, mindful of her responsibilities to the rest of the pack and particularly to her remaining three cubs, she got herself together and again assumed her duties as a leader and a mother.

It was snowing now just like it had when Miya died, and Dakar began thinking about how he had tried to keep her warm on cold mornings like this. He remembered lying beside her and trying to give her as much warmth as he could. Dakar had felt the loss of Miya as deeply as did his mother. Dakar's brother, Tagar, and his other sister, Pika, had teased her unmercifully. Dakar had always been her protector and champion. He had felt immensely protective towards her and tried never to be far from her side. He wondered, *Since I was so successful in protecting her from other animals, how could something unseen kill her so easily?* He was constantly being reminded how much of the world he still didn't understand.

As the pack exited the heavy timber to hunt in the open fields for game, a pile of snow dropped off the overhanging branches of a Pacific yew tree onto the leader of the pack, Dakar's father, Torga. The snow covered the huge Canadian timber wolf's back and made the deep black of Torga's coat look even blacker. Dakar tried to hold back his laughter and kept it all in except for one playful snort. His father was normally very gentle, but he had a short temper whenever he led the pack on a hunt.

Torga shook his heavy winter coat of fur, which had such a thick undercoat this time of year that it made him look almost as large as a bear. Torga was so large and powerful that no other wolves in the pack ever challenged him.

It was snowing heavily, and the air smelled fresh and clean to Dakar. Also, the snow dampened most of the sounds, so the forest was strangely quiet. Dakar's sister, Pika, playfully nipped his tail from her position behind him.

"Stop that, Pika!" Dakar admonished. "You're going to get me in trouble. You know how father is when we're on a hunt. This is one time that father doesn't allow us to get away with any playing!"

At that moment, Torga looked around, his huge head bristling with long black hair flecked with fresh snow. His golden amber eyes glowed with anger. "Hush," he growled. "You want to eat, don't you? There's a herd of caribou up ahead, and if you two scare them off, you're going to have to chase them back here. It isn't summer yet, and we still can't afford to use more energy than we have to. You're old enough to have a sense of responsibility to the pack. Use it!"

Dakar bowed his head in submission. He hated to have his father scold him. He admired his father so, and he hoped one day to be the pack leader, but his father constantly told him that the leadership had to be earned by respect of the rest of the pack. Torga didn't give Dakar as much leeway as he gave the other cubs. Dakar, after all, meant "chosen one" in wolf language, and Torga expected Dakar to live up to his name. *I don't want to do anything to upset the hunt,* he thought. *Besides going hungry, I'd lose face.* He snarled at Pika, but didn't say anything, lest he anger his father further.

Dakar noticed that Torga stiffened and held perfectly still, his ears alert and pointed forward. Torga's eyes locked on movement far in front of him. His guard hairs stood stiffly up on his back above his shoulders; his body quivered in anticipation of the hunt.

The remainder of the pack immediately followed Torga's lead and abruptly halted all movement. Just before following Torga's signal, Tanya quickly glanced questioningly at Dakar and Pika to be sure they understood the seriousness of the hunt about to take place. Satisfied, she turned to face the same direction as Torga, and she likewise stiffened.

Dakar's sense of smell had not yet fully developed, so he had not smelled the prey until that moment. It was a source of wonder to Dakar that Torga could sometimes smell prey as far away as several miles. Dakar looked in the direction Torga was staring, and he could barely make out the shapes of twenty caribou across the open meadow a quarter of a mile away. Their light tan color, mingled with patches of snow clinging to their skin, blended with the snow-covered forest behind them.

5

Torga slowly turned to Tanya, and said, "Take Maya, Surle, and Halwa, together with the cubs, around in front of the herd and run them back to this side. Mutar and I will be waiting here. Take your time getting around them. In this snowfall, they are more likely to smell you than to see you, so be sure to stay downwind." Dakar knew that it was Torga's favorite attack plan to send the lighter, faster females around to chase the prey towards the heavier, stronger males. The males would then grab the intended prey while the rest of the pack caught up and helped finish the kill. Dakar was proud of his father's wisdom and planning skills. He and the other two cubs always went with their mother. Later, when Dakar and Tagar were older, they would join the adult males.

Dakar saw that the caribou were busy eating "old-man's beard," a lichen that draped the trees in the spruce grove next to them. The caribou had interrupted a flock of "winter finches" that had sought harbor in the spruce trees to ride out the storm, and the sound of the birds chattering as they sought shelter further in the grove insured that any noise the wolves made would go unnoticed.

Tanya led her group along the timber on her side of the meadow with well-practiced precision. The wolves ambled along gracefully, as though they were hardly moving.

Tanya turned to Dakar and spoke in a hushed voice, "Stay right behind me and follow my lead exactly. It's time for you to learn how to lead a hunt, because soon it will be your place."

Dakar was astonished, for he had never before been invited to be in such an honored position. He vowed not to disappoint his parents. He proudly took his place behind his mother with his tail held erect and his ears pointing forward. His grey and white coat seemed to thicken with pride, as the long hair along his back raised with excitement.

The wolves circled carefully around the edge of the timber. The wind was in their face, so their scent wouldn't be carried toward the prey in front of them. Following Tanya's lead, they entered the forest several hundred yards before getting to the caribou. Now, Tanya lowered her body as she crept through the forest. The shadows filtering through the trees cast eerie lines across the snow, camouflaging the animals even more. Only the frosty breath of the stalking wolves seemed to move. Tanya advanced very slowly towards the prey, every muscle taunt and ready to leap should the herd sound the alarm.

The other six wolves stalked in an orderly line right behind Tanya, following her every move in well-practiced precision; their lives depended on being successful in the hunt. Dakar realized the urgency of this hunt. Game was not plentiful, and three wolf cubs increased dramatically the amount of food the pack needed to survive.

Just before the hunters broke through the timber, Tanya gave the signal to spread out, and the pack got side by side with Dakar right next to his mother. Then, in an explosion of movement, the wolves charged forward right at the caribou herd.

Dakar saw, as he bolted forward, that the caribou bleated and jumped about in terror. The caribou thundered away from the charging wolves, running with all their speed. The sight of the predators suddenly bursting out of the forest panicked the caribou and made their escape disorganized.

As the caribou approached Torga and Mutar, the two waiting wolves lay down in the snow with their ears tightly against their head; they folded their tails under them so that only their fierce amber eyes disclosed their location. The caribou were almost upon them when Torga noticed one old female faltering to the side, and he instantly grunted, "Now!"

Immediately he jumped towards the old caribou with Mutar right beside him. Torga jumped at her face and bit down on her nose with all his immense strength. He held on until she stumbled, then Mutar grabbed her left hind leg and pulled it out from under her. Before she could get back up, the remainder of the pack arrived, and they finished the kill.

Torga, of course, got his choice of the meal first. Then, in precise order, Tanya, Mutar, Maya, Surle, and Halwa took their turns. Although it was now Dakar's turn, Pika, his sister, jumped in and grabbed a piece of the leg first. Since she already possessed the meat, she was allowed to keep it by wolf tradition. Dakar didn't want to needlessly assert himself, anyway. There was plenty of meat for all. He only growled, "Pika, don't make a habit of doing that. I'll let it go just this once."

Pika whimpered, turning her head sideways and looking at Dakar. "Sorry, brother. I forget sometimes. I'm just *so* hungry."

Tanya heard the exchange and glanced over at her son. "You did a good job today, Dakar. I'm proud of you. In no time, you'll be joining your father and Mutar." Dakar smiled proudly, walked over, and licked his mother's mouth, giving her wolf kisses.

Torga quit eating long enough to say, "Maybe on the next hunt you will join Mutar and me. We'll see how you do. With summer coming on, I'm going to be busy protecting Tanya and her next set of cubs. It's time for you to take over some responsibility."

This day, which had started off so badly, was beginning to be the most wonderful day in Dakar's life! He was so happy he started dancing in circles and licking all the members of the pack. Several of the older ones growled, annoyed by Dakar's interruption of their wonderful meal, but their growls were more irritation than anger. They all realized that one day they would be following Dakar.

Pika, having finished eating, came over to Dakar with her head and tail down. "I'm sorry I ate before you, brother dear," she said. When Dakar turned to her, she licked his mouth, then lay down with her legs stretched out.

Dakar licked her neck, saying, "It's all right, little sister. There's plenty for all. I know you grabbed before you thought. Be sure it doesn't happen again, though," he added with a smile.

Full at last, the pack huddled in the snow next to their kill to digest the meal and rest from the hunt. They knew that if they left the kill, some other animals would quickly finish it. They therefore would not travel far from the site until they had completely devoured the rest of the caribou. They each went over to Torga and Tanya and licked the leaders' mouths in homage, then lay down for a well-deserved nap.

CHAPTER 2

The pack slept for several hours, until around noon. While they slept the snowfall had ceased, and the sky had cleared, making the snow soft and slushy. Suddenly, Torga jumped up, instantly alert. His quick reaction and tenseness stirred the remainder of the pack. As the other wolves looked around to find the source of Torga's alarm, Dakar stared at his father. He admired and loved the huge but gentle leader. Torga weighed about 160 pounds; extremely large, even for a wolf. Dakar weighed only 100 pounds, but his structure held the promise that one day he would be as large as his father. Torga looked in every direction, sensing rather than seeing some danger to the pack. He had heard something that was out of rhythm with the quiet serenity of the after-kill calm. The fresh smell of the recent kill again excited the pack, even though they were temporarily full.

Soon, a slight hum filled the air, almost as faint as a fly's droning, except this hum got increasingly louder. Soon, it resembled thunder. However, it didn't die out, but rather got louder and louder. Confused, the wolf pack circled round and

DAKAR, A WOLF'S ADVENTURE

round in an attempt to locate the source of the strange noise. Dakar was puzzled. He had never heard anything so loud, and he had no idea where the sound came from.

Suddenly, a shadow appeared on the snow, and Dakar saw Torga look up in the sky. Dakar followed his father's glance, and he saw a strange metal bird similar to the ones he had occasionally seen the previous summer flying high over the park in Canada that was home to the pack. They had unwittingly been the beneficiaries of a protected environment where hunting for wolves was illegal.

Dakar had never seen the metal birds this close to the ground. It was making a terrifying noise, and the pack started yelping in frustration and fear, for they did not have any idea what danger this object presented. Dakar and the pack were more afraid of the unknown than any danger they could measure.

The metal bird started circling around the meadow, descending in altitude with each circle. The wolves were now torn between their fear of the object and their desire to protect their kill. As the metal bird got lower, Dakar could see through the glass on the sides that the object contained the dreaded humans.

Dakar had never actually seen a human up close. Last summer, he had seen several walking through the woods at a distance, but Torga told him never to get close to one if he could help it. Dakar remembered that Torga told him they were the most dangerous beings in the forest.

At that moment, Torga growled, "We have to leave the kill. I sense trouble. Follow me into the woods." He then took off through the snow towards a stand of thick Engelmann spruce on the opposite side of the meadow. Dakar understood his father's tactic; the thick cover of the spruce would give the pack the maximum shelter available. The pack followed Torga as he bounded through the snow, desire to protect the pack giving him extra power to struggle through the white slush. Mutar followed him closely, with the adult females coming right behind. Tanya, worried about her cubs, waited while Pika and Tagar tried to fight their way through the mushy snow. Dakar had joined the adults, not realizing that his weaker brother and sister would have difficulty tramping through the snow.

Dakar noticed that the metal bird, which was outfitted with skis under its wheels, knew the path the wolves were taking and had altered its course to cut them off. The metal bird was rapidly descending on its path in front of the spruce grove, and

Dakar could feel the wind from the displaced air under the metal bird, and he could smell the unfamiliar pungent odor of gasoline. The contrast between the calm of the post-hunt nap and the race for safety from an unexpected threat created panic throughout the pack. Dakar could tell they were just going to reach the safety of the trees before the metal bird touched the snow, and then he realized he didn't see his mother or his brother or sister in front of him. Torga had just entered the spruce grove and the flying snow together with the rising steam from five heavily breathing wolves had obscured Dakar's ability to know who was in front and who was not.

Dakar glanced quickly behind him and was alarmed to discover that his mother and siblings were about twenty yards behind; Tanya would not leave her cubs. Dakar yelped, "Hurry! You've got to hurry, or you won't make it before that thing hits ground!" Dakar knew they would never make it, that the dreaded machine would cut off their path to the safety of the timber.

Dakar knew his father had a responsibility to the whole pack, that he couldn't endanger all the adults because of his family. Dakar realized it was up to him to help his mother. At this time, his only responsibility was to his family. If he was to ever deserve leadership, he couldn't abandon those he loved now. He quickly made his decision. He got to the edge of the grove, concealed himself behind some "butterwort" bushes and "white lady's slippers" plants and waited to see what he should do. Torga had taken the remainder of the pack further into the safety of the timber.

The metal bird landed and wind from the propeller scattered some of the snow that hadn't begun to melt in puffs of white powder, eliminating any chance of observing the whereabouts of Tanya and the cubs.

As the snow dust cleared, Dakar could see four men depart from the right side of the metal bird, closest to him. They all had beards, and he could smell their foul odor, a smell he would always hate. They were dressed in down jackets, with down-filled covers over their pants. They had high fur-lined boots with rubber soles. Dakar observed that they each had a long metal object in their hands that they obviously treasured. They were each carrying their objects in both hands very carefully. One of the humans, a large, heavyset monster, gathered the others and said, "We've got three of them cut off. Henry, you, Ben, and Jacque go around to the right. I'll go to the left of the plane, and we'll have them cut off from the pack.

We won't get the whole pack, but we will have something to show for the trip. I told you we could poach here this time of year without any problems. The wardens don't expect anyone to come here now. Let's be quick about it, though. No sense hanging around, asking for trouble." Dakar didn't know what the human was saying, but he could tell by the tone of his voice that he meant harm to the wolves. The human's face was drawn in a scowl, a sign that Dakar *did* understand. The crunching of the poachers' boots on the wet snow was an ominous punctuation to the horrible scene emerging.

Dakar had no experience with a problem like this. He wanted to help his family, but he didn't know exactly what danger these strangers presented, or how to overcome them. His frustration caused his heart to beat faster and his breath to come in rapid, short bursts. Every part of his body was tuned to the scene before him as he crouched in the snow, ready to act as soon as he knew what to do.

The poachers trodded steadily around the metal bird, their boots making loud plopping noises as they hit the wet snow. Dakar could tell they were walking towards his family as they converged on the other side. Dakar could see underneath the metal bird's body. He could see Tanya and his siblings in front

17

of the hunters, confused and cut off from the rest of the pack and the safety of the woods. His heart went out to the plight of his loved ones, and he could imagine the horror and anxiety they felt; the intruders were blocking any chance of returning to the pack. The determined, sinister look on the hunters' faces served to heighten the intensity of Dakar's emotions, as he wondered what he could do to save his family.

Suddenly, he saw the largest man raise the metal object to his shoulder, and suddenly the quiet was shattered by an explosion that rattled Dakar's attention, and he immediately smelled the foul intense odor of gunpowder. He would never forget that smell as long as he lived. He knew right away that he had witnessed the reason Torga had told him that humans were so dangerous. He saw a puff of snow pop up from the surface right next to his beloved mother, and Tanya jumped in front of Pika as the frightened mother emitted a soulful whine.

Dakar didn't stop to make any further plans; his family was in danger! He thrust himself forward with all his power, ran right under the metal bird, and catapulted himself right into the back of the human who had caused the explosion. As he did, he let out a deep snarl that made the other humans jump with fear and start running. The heavy snow did not allow them to run very far before Dakar, whose feet were large and designed to move through the snow, jumped into the back of Ben, knocking him into Jacque, who hit Henry in a domino effect. The poachers all were scurrying about in the snow, trying to protect themselves from the unexpected attack and stumbling into each other as they attempted to retrieve their weapons.

While the poachers were still indecisive about their next move, Dakar turned to his mother, saying, "Quickly, take the cubs to the pack. I'll keep these animals busy long enough for you to make it. Go!"

Tanya looked with pride at Dakar for an instant, then gruffed, "Be careful, my hero," as she sped for the safety of the forest with the cubs right behind her.

Dakar then whirled right back over the prostrate humans to keep them down and off-balance. He sensed that they would be ineffective if they weren't on their feet. He used a technique that wolves used to intimidate each other; growling and baring his enormous teeth, with his ears forward and his tail straight up in the air in a dominant position. The long hairs on his back were raised, making him look even larger and more intimidating. When he realized that he had gone as far as he

19

could with that tactic, he looked towards the forest and made sure the cubs had entered the safety of the trees. He then ran as fast as he could in the opposite direction, which was south. He hoped he had so angered the humans that they would follow him rather than go after the pack. He would lead them far away from the pack before losing them and circling to find his family. His fear and anger gave him the strength he needed to keep up his pace and make the safety of the cedar and hemlock timber long before the poachers could mount any effective counterattack. He was huffing so hard he could feel his lungs pressing against the resistance of his ribs. His condensed breath partially blocked his view in front, so that he had to turn his head to the side to see clearly. The fresh smell of the forest helped to revitalize him and give him some comfort. He now had time to reflect on his actions, and he admitted he was proud of himself. He had faced his first real challenge, and he had proven himself up to the task. He had saved his loved ones. He knew his position in the pack would be different now, and he would no longer just be one of the cubs. Now, he had to elude the hunters, keep them away from his family, then find his way back to the pack.

Dakar's thoughts abruptly returned to his predicament when he heard the sounds of crunching in the snow signaling the pursuit of the poachers. Dakar got very low and turned, looking out from behind a cedar tree towards the sounds of the pursuers. He saw that only two of them were following him. He soon understood why, as he heard the awful sound of the metal machine starting up, and he saw the shapes of the other two poachers in the window of the machine. He realized his task of keeping the hunters away from the pack might not be completed; those terrible humans may be going after the pack again. He must make them follow him! He rose from his hiding place, allowing the two pursuers to see him before he turned and ran again toward the south. He knew that if they followed him, he would be going in the opposite direction from the pack. He couldn't plan beyond that.

He heard one of the hunters shouting, "Ben, I see him over by that cedar grove. Let's spread out, and we'll get him when he tries to return to the pack." Dakar didn't know what the hunters were saying, but he knew they had seen him and were attempting to follow him. Dakar kept running south, and he was soon in unfamiliar territory. He could hear the hunters relentlessly trudging behind, and he knew he had

21

accomplished his task of making them angry enough to follow him rather than the pack. It occurred to him that he should have killed several of them, but he had not been taught to kill except for food. He knew the hunters had no such reservations, and he realized he might have to kill in order to survive. His father had always handled protection of the pack; now he was learning that it might be necessary to kill for protection. He hated the humans that had disturbed his wonderful day and made him start thinking about killing. He was now in strange country, and he was confused as to the proper course of action. He missed his family and his pack. He wanted to lie down somewhere and whimper, but he had work to do.

*   *   *

John, the pilot of the plane, was frustrated and angry. He had promised his clients they would get some wolf trophies. They had made it plain they were not bothered by breaking some regulations in order to get the trophies, and they had made it clear they would pay a good price, but only if they were successful. John had seen this pack of wolves from the air several times, and he knew they must stay pretty much in this part of the Kootenay National Park. He had also seen this herd of caribou several days ago, and he knew they would be irresistible to the wolves during the lean spring months, before the snow melted. For one thing, they were easier prey than the moose the wolves would otherwise choose to hunt, and they were not quite as big or hard to trap. He had been sure, when he saw the pack relaxing after a kill, that it would be an easy $7,500. He already had planned how he was going to spend it. He had three great trophies lined up, and now this one wolf had spoiled it for him. He was going to get him, no matter what. Now, it was revenge. He knew his French-Canadian guide, Jacque, felt the same way. Jacque never wanted anything to get in the way of his whiskey and his women.

He turned to Henry, the client in the plane with him. "Too bad my foot slipped when I took that shot at the she-wolf. If I'd hit her, you two could have each gotten your wolf trophy and be ready to go back to Oklahoma."

"Yeah, well, maybe Ben can get that durn wolf that spoiled it for us. Never knew a wolf would have the nerve to jump us like that," Henry replied.

Humm, at least we'd get $2,500 for our day's work. That wouldn't be a bad day, and we'd have our revenge in the bargain, John thought.

"I think I'll try to find a landing place in front of the wolf, then you'll get a shot at him, if Ben doesn't get him."

John took the plane over to the location where he had seen the wolf and his companions enter the woods. If he could find a landing place somewhere in front, they would have the wolf cornered.

John saw a level spot between the Kootenay River and the forest through which the wolf and his pursuers were traveling. If the wolf continued on his southerly course, he would come out of the forest right into this clearing. John turned the plane so as to land lengthwise along the path by the river and began to descend.

"Look, there by the trees!" Henry exclaimed. "There's that wolf just coming out of the timber, at the top of that slope!"

*   *   *

Dakar heard the plane overhead, and he sensed the plan of the hunters. He knew that the flying object could touch down on land, and the humans inside could get out, as they had done before. He knew he had to hurry, for he didn't want to deal with both the hunters behind and the humans in the metal bird. The terrain started sloping uphill, and he knew that was good, because the pursuers would have a more difficult climb than he. He could hear their labored breathing, and he knew he didn't have too far to go before they would be unable to keep up. However, he could feel his energy lagging also, and his breathing was more difficult. He entered a heavy stand of Douglas fir and lodgepole pine, which gave him added cover. Soon, he was at the top of the incline, and he saw a river down below.

As he contemplated his next move, he heard the dreaded sound of the metal bird. He assumed they had seen him, and he saw them descending to an open meadow between him and the river. He was tired and dejected. These humans seemed to be everywhere. Somehow, he *had* to get past them.

He understood that if they were successful, they would cut him off, and his chances of escape would be diminished considerably. He thought for a minute and decided he would have to take a chance. He knew they would never be able to cross the river. While it had a lot of ice in it, it was not completely frozen over, and he sensed that they would not be able to swim with the heavy clothing they wore. He dashed downhill with the snow flying in the air on both sides of him, as if he were waterskiing. He no longer worried about

25

concealment; he only wanted to make the river before the hunters could get out of the metal bird.

The plane hit ground just as Dakar was about to enter the river. First, Henry jumped out, then John hurdled out of his door, the dreaded loud engine still running. Dakar could see Henry putting that horrible metal stick to his shoulder out of the corner of his eye.

Just as Dakar leaped for the water, he heard the awful booming sound he had heard earlier, and he immediately felt a burning sensation in his shoulder. He hit the water, went under the surface for a second, and then rose to the top. The frigid water helped ease the burning in his shoulder, and it also made his exhausted body come alive. He knew he could not stay in the water long, so he struggled to get to the other side with all the strength he had remaining. Soon, he reached the other side, pulled himself slowly out of the water behind some willows, and lay down to assess his condition.

He looked across the river and saw the two hunters who had gotten out of the metal bird standing on the banks of the river. Both of them had their dreaded metal sticks up to their shoulders. They were looking down the sticks, and soon Dakar heard the terrible sounds again. He saw snow kicking up near him, and he remembered the snow popping up around Tanya before he had attacked the hunters. He cautiously crawled away from the river, being sure to keep concealment between him and the hunters. He found a grove of thick cedars several hundred feet from the river, and the hunters were nowhere to be seen. He felt he could safely rest here for a while. His shoulder was starting to stiffen. He lay down on the snow in a tight knot and contemplated his next move. His shoulder was hurting terribly, and he had no idea where he was. He *so* missed the warm touch of his mother's body beside him and the reassuring gruff of his father's voice.

CHAPTER 3

As soon as Tanya and the cubs rejoined the rest of the pack, Torga led them steadily northward and a little west upslope towards Foster Peak, on the westerly edge of the park. Torga knew this area, and he was confident that the humans would not be able to follow the pack up there. He had seen humans near here, but not this early in the year. The steep slopes and unstable snow would discourage all but the hardiest of humans; these poachers did not appear to meet those qualifications.

They plodded carefully but steadily upward, still cautious lest the hunters surprise them and attempt to follow. They trekked through a dense Engelmann spruce and subalpine fir forest with scattered stands of pine and alpine larch. The tension the pack felt was contradicted by the sound of the boreal chickadees along the route, happy that spring was coming and the snow had stopped for the day. They saw a group of blue grouse cross their path. Normally the wolves would break ranks and chase the birds just to vent energy.

Torga saw that the some of the pack were looking at the grouse with anticipation. "No one is to leave the pack. We have to be careful, even up here. We aren't sure where that metal bird is, or where it might appear," Torga warned.

"When do you think it'll be safe to go and look for Dakar?" Tanya asked anxiously.

"Later today. I'm sure he's trying to lead the humans away from us. That's what I'd do." Tanya had told him of Dakar's exploits, and he was worried about Dakar's fate. His responsibility to the pack prevented any attempt to return and search for Dakar now. If Dakar survived, they would find him when it was safe. Torga scent-marked the route along the way, both to warn other wolves of their presence and to give Dakar a map as to their whereabouts. They had not crossed the boundary of any other wolf pack along the way, so they didn't have to worry about a clash. It was the rule that packs stay within their own boundaries. Torga knew that most of packs around this part of the country were further north. This is why he had picked this location for his pack.

Tanya came up to Torga, and said pleadingly, "Torga, can't we go look for Dakar? After all, he saved my life and the lives of your children. We've never been this far from our territory. He'll never find us! Can't we help him? He was *so* brave!"

Torga looked compassionately at her and said, "Tanya, I've got seven other lives to think about. If it were just I, I'd go help Dakar in an instant. Don't forget, he took this course of action so the pack could get away. He was thinking like a leader, and that's what I have to do. You'll never know how much I want to help him. I love him and am proud of him, too. After all, it's rare that a leader can know his son will probably be the next leader of the pack. As soon as it's safe, we'll go back down and look for him. Don't worry." Torga had to focus his senses on any potential threat; he couldn't allow himself to be distracted with any other thoughts, including the pride he felt for his son. That would come later. Now, he had to maintain discipline in the pack, use his urine to mark their route, and be ready for any danger that appeared.

Tanya left Torga alone after their discussion. She was busy taking care of Pika and Tagar. It was the first time they had ever been in any serious danger, and they were having trouble dealing with it. "Tanya, you've got to keep Pika and Tagar from whining," Torga said. "The welfare of the pack requires that they keep quiet." "I will," she said. She looked at the two cubs, and they hung their heads. "Cubs, this isn't play. The safety of the pack depends on every one of us. Do your part." The two cubs nodded in compliance. Torga had heard nothing to alarm him since shortly after they had begun their escape, when he had heard the metal bird take off. He stopped, turned, and said to the pack, "We'll rest for awhile. Then, I'll see if it's time to backtrack and look for Dakar."

Tanya smiled with relief, walked over, licked Torga's mouth, and said, "Thank you."

*   *   *

Dakar awoke with a startle. He had slept for several hours. He could tell he had been seriously injured, for his shoulder was sore and hot. When he tried to stretch his left front leg, it moved grudgingly. He was still tired, and he knew that he wouldn't have been able to run much further; he was lucky the river served as a barrier to protect him from the humans. He saw that the noise that startled him was only that of a mountain bluebird. It was the first he had seen since last fall, and he hoped that was a good omen. The lilting song of the bird, together with the fresh smell of the pine needles, soothed him. However, he knew he had better be constantly aware, in case the hunters were still around. That metal bird could come down anywhere. He understood that they were not going to be easily discouraged. He had made them angry, and they obviously held a grudge. He decided that he could not look for the pack while there was a chance the hunters were still on his trail. He certainly didn't want to undo the good he had done by leading the hunters back to the pack. He therefore had no choice but to continue going away from the territory of the pack until he knew it was safe to return.

Dakar now understood fully what a crucial decision he had made when he had charged the hunters and then led them away. It might be days before he could rejoin the pack, if at all. Suddenly, he felt very sad. His days with the pack and his siblings had been full of joy and contentment. He had a loving mother, father, and aunts and uncles. He had not been required to make any important decisions on his own before. It was all because of those humans! Now, he hated them with all his being. He felt he now could kill them if he had the chance. He hated them even more for making him have such thoughts at a time when he would otherwise be celebrating the beginning of spring and the end of a difficult winter, where hunger was a part of life.

He decided to strike out along the river and head south. At least that way he would have a way to gauge where he started from when he decided to head back and find his family. Also, if the hunters got on his side of the river, he could always cross back over, so he had that avenue of escape. He did, of course, scent-mark his route.

It was now mid-afternoon, and Dakar decided to go as far as he could before nightfall, so he would lessen the chances that the hunters would be able to pursue him. He got into a steady pace, and the terrain was relatively easy to negotiate. The only sounds he heard during his journey were those of the "winter finches" warbling in the trees and the ducks he scared as he walked up on them. He stopped once to watch an American dipper dive into the river and completely submerge before reappearing with a small fish in its mouth. If he had been in a different mood, he would have stayed and watched the curious bird for a while, but he knew he couldn't let down his guard.

It was starting to get dark, and he knew he had to find a safe place to spend the night. He found a hollowed tree trunk about one hundred feet from the river, secluded in a fir thicket. He upset a family of squirrels that had made the trunk their home, but he was in no mood to chase squirrels, and he was not hungry. Besides, his shoulder was hurting worse, and he could feel it stiffening. He could see that the wound was still bleeding, and his walking kept it irritated. He knew he shouldn't be walking until it healed, but he had no choice. He curled up inside the trunk. He had covered around thirty miles, traveling at a pace of around five miles an hour.

CHAPTER 4

Torga saw that the pack was well rested. The trek had not been particularly demanding for the wolf pack. Torga remembered times during the fall when they had traveled one hundred miles searching for food before the snow came. He could see that Tanya was getting increasingly edgy; she was very worried about Dakar. It had been half a day since the encounter with the hunters, and he knew that either Dakar had eluded them by now, or something he didn't want to think about had happened.

"Let's start back, but I want you all to listen, smell, and watch in every direction. I don't think those humans followed us up here, but they may have sense enough to go back to the kill. That's where it'll get really dangerous," Torga stated.

Tanya started licking Torga's mouth in excitement, for she now was getting to look for her beloved Dakar. "What do you think Dakar did after we left?" Tanya asked hesitantly.

"I would think he'll be smart enough to try to keep those humans away from the kill, if he can," Torga replied. "He wouldn't take the risk he took and then not think about the welfare of the pack, but we don't know what happened after we left. After all, there were four humans," Torga delicately answered, knowing that the odds of an inexperienced young wolf eluding four humans weren't good.

Tanya was very quiet for a few moments, then she said, "I don't think I could handle losing another one of my cubs. I still miss Miya terribly. I *know* how dangerous it was for Dakar to do what he did to save our lives."

"All we can do now is go back to the meadow. Then, we'll know what happened. Right now I've got to make sure we're all safe on the way back. I'm worried about Dakar, too, but I have to think about everyone else at the same time."

The path back was relatively easy. The pack had already blazed a trail through the snow, and they were traveling downhill, so they made excellent time. The sun was now out, and the mountain chickadees and the bluebirds were singing happily, announcing the beginning of the spring season. It was a dramatic contrast to the intensity of determination Torga felt to unite his pack and his family.

They approached the spruce grove they had entered to escape the hunters, and the vile smell of the sweat and lotion of the hunters still invaded the air, vividly bringing the perilous escape back to mind. Torga could also still smell the pungent gasoline odor that was so foreign to the pure air of the mountains.

"We're getting close. Walk like you were stalking a deer. We can't take any chances!" Torga whispered to the pack. The pack immediately slumped into a low, stalking posture as they moved forward one slow step at a time. They finally were able to see the meadow, and thankfully, there were no bodies visible, except for the kill.

Torga looked through the "avalanche lilies" and "white spring beauties" that grew on the edge of the forest, and he could smell nothing but the remains of the encounter: the gasoline, the sweat mingled with fear that the humans left in the air, and the faint scent of Dakar's footprints. He didn't pick up any recent smells, which told him Dakar and the hunters had departed long ago.

"There's no sign of Dakar or the humans. And no sign that anyone was injured!" he said with relief as he slowly turned towards Tanya's expectant face. He smiled at her as her face softened into the loveliest smile he had seen in many hours. Her amber eyes softened as she licked his mouth, and he was aware that no wolf could have a more loyal, courageous, or more beautiful mate. Now, if they could just find Dakar safe, everything would be perfect.

At Torga's signal, all the wolves slowly lay down under the cover of the lilies to wait until they could hear, smell, or sense any activity in the area and to satisfy themselves that no trap was present. They all knew that safety resided in patience. After about twenty minutes of motionless searching Torga finally rose, and the pack slowly descended to the site of the confrontation with the hunters. The scent of Dakar was intermingled with that of the hunters, and then Dakar's footprints led towards the other end of the meadow. Torga understood Dakar's tactic, and he smiled with pride. Dakar would be a worthy pack leader when his time came. Torga could feel the coolness of the setting sun, and he realized that it would be dark before too long. Under the circumstances, he did not feel they should travel at night. He had no idea where the humans were and what tools they had for operating under cover of darkness. He had long since learned that humans had implements to do a variety of things, and he had also learned to expect the worse.

"Tanya, take the pack to the caribou carcass and let them have a good meal. Then we'll den up for the night somewhere away from the kill, where it's safe. We'll get started in the morning on Dakar's trail," Torga said gently.

"Do you have any idea where Dakar is?" Tanya asked apprehensively.

"I know what he's doing. He's leading the hunters away from us. We'll be able to pick up his trail tomorrow. Don't worry."

Tanya started to say something, obviously decided that Torga had enough on his mind, and walked toward the caribou with the pack right behind her. Torga walked over to Dakar's tracks, followed them for a while, and made note that two of the hunters were in pursuit of Dakar. He also wondered where the other two were.

*   *   *

John Sanders was angry and exasperated. He had let Henry Winslow take the shot at the wolf, so he could collect $2,500. That was the fee agreed upon for every wolf the clients got. He knew the clients would feel cheated if he had killed the wolf and then tried to collect the fee. He didn't know why Winslow wanted to hunt wolves so bad, if he couldn't hit one at thirty yards. Now, the wolf had temporarily gotten the best of them. He didn't want to talk to Winslow, because he knew he would say something that would cost him some money. He definitely didn't want to do that. Fortunately, right then Jacque and Ben Tunnell arrived.

Jacque looked questioningly at John for a moment, then said, "It's obvious you didn't get him. How could you miss? He was headed right this way, Mon Cher."

Winslow chimed in, "I took a shot at him, but he jumped into the river just as I shot. Otherwise, I'd have gotten him for sure."

Jacque Tremaine looked inquisitively at Sanders, who raised an eyebrow in disbelief but didn't say anything. The corner of Tremaine's mouth curled up in a slight contemptuous smile.

Tunnell was puffing so hard that Tremaine walked over to him, and said condescendingly, "Listen, sit down for a while. We aren't about to cross that river anyway. Not without the plane. You did your best, but I think you've gone about as far as you can today."

Tunnell gratefully sat down, and said with determination, "I want that wolf. I'm not about to let one little scrawny wolf get the best of me. I don't know about you, but Henry, I'm willing to raise the ante and guarantee these guys $2,000, win or lose. After all, we're big people in Oklahoma. How would it look?" Winslow only nodded his head slowly in confirmation.

Sanders was trying to decide whether to continue, then he noticed a strange smell. He glanced at Tunnell and wondered, *How does Tunnell manage to smell so badly? Doesn't the man ever bathe? I thought Jacque was untidy, but here's a new champion. Oh well, in this job we won't get the pick of the litter.*

Sanders thought a moment more, and then he said, "Well, $2,000 will get you another full day out here. Let's head back to Calgary and get a fresh start first thing tomorrow morning. I'm afraid you all aren't in shape to do the kind of tracking we'd have to do today. With a fresh start early tomorrow, we'll have plenty of daylight to find that wolf's tracks from the air and figure out where he is before we land and get him on foot. With a little luck, we won't even have to walk far." Winslow and Tunnell only nodded their agreement.

CHAPTER 5

Dakar, weary and sore, slept fitfully through the night. It was the first night he had ever spent away from his parents and his pack. He really missed having the warm bodies of his family beside him. His shoulder was hurting badly, and he noticed that his skin was hot. He could feel that there was some foreign substance lodged in the wound. The sun was shining, and the warmth of the rays increased the heat he felt from his injury. He slowly stretched, licked at his wound, and then stiffly stood to get a drink of water. It hurt even to walk over to the river. Each step brought a bolt of pain. He heard the early morning melody of the bluebirds, which his mother loved so much, and he realized how much he wished he were back home with his loved ones.

"I thought you would never wake up! It's time to get on our way!" said a voice on top of the tree trunk Dakar was using as a temporary den.

Dakar quickly looked up and saw a large raven atop the trunk. The large raven's coal black feathers seemed to glow in the morning light. "Are you talking to me? I don't know you. Who are you?" Dakar questioned.

"My good fellow has a lot of questions for this early in the morning! First, I am talking to you, dummy. There's no one else around. Second, you *will* know me real well very soon. Third, my name is Rahwa. Next, I'm the one who's going to save your butt and find you someone to heal that infected shoulder of yours. That's enough questions, for a while."

"I don't understand. How in the world did you even know about my shoulder, and why would you want to help me?"

"I told you, no more questions. You may never know the answer to the questions you just asked, but you'd better just have faith in me. I'm here to help you, because you deserve to be helped. That's all you need to know. There is a time in everyone's life when he or she just has to have faith. This is your time. Trust me, and everything will turn out all right. Don't, and who knows? It's your call, my friend."

"I don't know anything about you. How can I possibly just put myself in your hands?"

I've got a family and a pack to think about, also. I wonder if I'm still sleeping and just dreaming. I don't know what my father would say to do. But, I sure do need somebody's help. This is something I haven't been taught to handle, he thought.

"Then, you'd better listen to your inner self. That is something you *have* been taught to do. I don't have all day. Make up your mind. You had a decision to make yesterday, and you decided to save your family. Now, you have another one that's just as important to you. What's it to be?"

"How in the world did you know about yesterday? This is the strangest conversation I've ever had. I haven't ever had a conversation with a bird before, come to think about it."

"Oh, I'm much more than a bird, and I think before our trip is over, you'll know how I knew about yesterday. But that's up to you."

"Where would you take me?" Dakar asked as he sniffed the air, trying to get a sense of the energy Rahwa was releasing. Dakar had learned that he could often tell an animal's intentions by smelling certain types of odor given off by different emotions.

"Well, I'm going to take you south of here, to an Indian I know. He's got some herbs that will heal your shoulder properly. There's also a piece of metal lodged in your shoulder that has to come out. In addition, he and his friends will keep you safe from those hunters on your trail," answered Rahwa impatiently.

"I'd sure like to know how you know so much about me, but I guess you're not going to tell me that. I assume an Indian is a human, though, and I *hate* humans. I can't believe any of them would do anything but hurt me and those I love!"

"Well, you'll find this one is different from those you met yesterday. That's one of the things I want you to learn. That knowledge can save your life, and the lives of those you love. Either you're going to trust me, or not. What's it to be?"

I can't believe I'm doing this, but something deep inside me tells me to trust this whatever-he-is. Anyway, I don't see what I have to lose. I don't see how he can hurt me, Dakar thought. "You're right. I went with my instincts yesterday, and I did the right thing. I guess I'll stay with my instincts. I'll go along with you."

"Good call, Dakar! Let's be on our way! We're going to keep heading south, and we'll stay on the path right by the river. I'll be right overhead. Yell if you need anything."

Dakar wondered, *How in the world did he know my name? I didn't tell him!*

They had only traveled about an hour along the Kootenay River when it intersected with a new river. This river, the White River, angled east across Dakar's trail. Fortunately, it was mostly frozen over, but Dakar did have to get in the water for a few strokes. The cool water felt good to his feverish body, but it was difficult to stroke with his bad shoulder. It was not easy to get out of the river, for his shoulder was rapidly getting tighter and less useful.

"How goes it, Dakar?" asked Rahwa, who was standing on a rock on the other side of the river. He was casually preening his feathers as Dakar struggled out of the river.

"I have felt better, now that you mention it. I'm getting hungry, too. It's not going to be easy to catch any food with my shoulder as sore as it is," Dakar said. He curled his lip and let out a low growl in irritation at the lack of concern Rahwa displayed.

"Hey there, take it easy! No one said this trip was going to be easy. Here's where your decision to follow me pays its first dividends, 'ol buddy. There happens to be a couple of spruce grouse just around the next bend in the trail. They are about the slowest creatures I've ever seen. I'm sure you could catch them with just two good legs, never mind three. Also, I'll bet I can find some "midden heaps" the red squirrels have left around with their nuts cached for winter. I've seen a bunch of them as we've gone along."

"*Now* you're being helpful. I know what spruce grouse are. My father has gotten several of them for the pack when hunting is tough. Let's go!"

"Just be sure to leave some for me. I *love* to eat the scraps," Rahwa said with delight.

Dakar walked stealthily along the slight animal trail near the lake. The trail was really just a worn path in the snow that a succession of various animals had used throughout the winter. As Dakar rounded a turn, he saw the group of grouse. Overcoming the pain of his shoulder, he crouched. As the grouse started to run, Dakar sprung, activated by his hunger and the predatory instinct stimulated by an animal fleeing before him. Dakar, despite his injury, had no trouble catching the slow moving grouse. The smell of fresh food made him feel much better. He relaxed and settled down for an enjoyable meal.

"All right, piggy, where's my piece?" Rahwa said with a laugh. The shrill voice of the raven shattered Dakar's mood. "I didn't realize you were so hungry that you couldn't wait for me to at least have a bite or two. Here, I'll tear you off a piece. How can one little bitty bird *be* so much trouble?"

Rahwa cackled at Dakar's annoyance. "Listen, tough guy, before this trip is over, you'll wonder what you ever did before you met me. Remember I said that!"

"Okay, but how far are we going? My family is back on the mountain I left. I need to get back to them as soon as I can. I'm leaving a trail, but my father probably won't follow me. It might endanger the pack to leave our territory."

"At the rate you walk, the place we're going isn't more than a couple of days from here. We have to cross those mountains to the east, then we'll be there. As for the family, first things first. You're no good to anyone like you are, so let's get you fixed up. Then, you can worry about what to do with the rest of your life."

Dakar stared out over the river, toward home. He hadn't thought about the rest of his life since the hunters arrived. He longed to be home and safe.

After finishing their meal, the unlikely companions continued their journey. Rahwa flew about one hundred feet above Dakar in lazy circles, while Dakar kept his steady pace ever southward. The terrain was relatively easy to negotiate, although just to their east were the mountains that made up the continental divide, which separated British Columbia from the province of Alberta. The path they were using was now in a thin forest of Douglas fir, with huckleberry bushes, ferns, and rhododendrons scattered throughout making visibility difficult except in the direction of the river.

They had traveled about twenty miles when suddenly Dakar smelled an odor that made him immediately stop. He checked it again, and then as quietly as possible he called to Rahwa.

When Rahwa came down, Dakar said, "Well, now you've really gotten me in trouble. We're in the territory of another wolf pack! I just smelled their scent-mark, staking out their territory."

"So what? Do you know how huge this country is? There isn't anything around here for further than I can see way up there except the same trees and bushes you see here. Isn't there enough room for one little scraggly wolf to walk through here?" Rahwa said incredulously.

"You obviously don't understand wolf rules. A wolf pack stays in his territory and if he or she intrudes into another pack's territory, that pack either chases him out or he fights. It's a serious violation to cross another pack's territory."

"Geez. Now, on top of everything else, I've got to deal with macho wolf crap. Why can't everybody just get along and live and let live? You don't see birds up there in the air fighting for air to fly in, do you? Doesn't anyone understand that the land is meant to be used by whoever needs to use it, not hoarded like a carcass? If everyone takes care of it, it'll still be available for the next person. You're saying that if a wolf pack decides this is their piece of land, all other wolf packs have to go along with it? Doesn't that strike you as silly?"

"I never thought about it. It's just the rule," Dakar said timidly.

"See, you have more in common with humans than you want to admit. Humans think they can take the land and change it any way they want. They believe it belongs to them just because they have a piece of paper that says it does. Kinda like your scent-mark, I'd say," Rahwa said, as he puffed out his chest and looked at Dakar perceptively.

Dakar stared at Rahwa. He thought, *What is he trying to tell me? I just want to survive and get back to my family. I don't want to worry about any other problems.*

50

"Well, anyway, that is still my problem. How are you going to get me out of this one? I wouldn't have a chance against a wolf pack, even if I was healthy."

"Well, why don't we just see if we can make it through here without running into the pack? After all, we have the advantage. I'll be up in the air where I can see them long before they even know you're around. They don't have anything like that, now do they?"

"All right, but be sure to give me plenty of warning if you see them. I'll need all the head start I can get, with my shoulder and all."

"Aw, don't worry. The chances of us running into them are pretty small, with us just passing through, and all."

Sure, Dakar thought. *This raven doesn't know wolves as well as he thinks. We have a way of sensing when another is in our territory. I've seen father do it often enough.*

Reluctantly, Dakar rose and began to walk south at a steady pace, frequently stopping to sniff the air and listen for any howls that might identify the location of the resident pack. They continued the journey for about an hour more, with Dakar finding it increasingly difficult to maintain his pace with his sore shoulder. He longed for the luxury of just lying in the snow for a day, letting his body regain its strength.

Suddenly, Rahwa let out a loud screech and flew down to Dakar, landing right in front of him; Rahwa's eyes were dilated, and his little chest was heaving with every breath. "Oops, Dakar, I'm sorry, but there seems to be a pack of six wolves about two miles away over to the east past that hill."

Dakar looked in the direction Rahwa was describing. There was a rise of about one hundred fifty feet to the top of a hill covered in Englemann spruce and lodgepole pine. Dakar shuddered at the thought of the danger beyond that hill. He knew he couldn't outrun a healthy wolf pack, and he was far into their territory. He had no idea how far south their territory reached, so he didn't know if he could make it to the southern boundary before he was discovered. He realized he was in a very perilous situation.

"Rahwa, is this what trusting you gets me? I'm in a more dangerous situation now than I was when we met! I thought you were going to help solve my problems, not get me into trouble."

"Don't worry, my friend. I've got a trick or two up my wings. I've got a plan, and I think it will work."

Dakar hoped very much that he was right to trust Rahwa. Right now, his life depended on that decision being correct.

CHAPTER 6

Torga allowed the pack to eat as much as they could, for he knew they would be going into unfamiliar territory in their search for Dakar. He also ate until he could eat no more. It was a nervous dinner, for all the pack was on guard in case the hunters should still be in the area. Afterwards, Torga took the pack to their den area up in the redcedar and hemlock forest several miles from the kill site. It had been a long day, and Torga knew that Tanya would want to start on their search early the next morning.

Torga knew that Tanya was thinking about Dakar. He realized that she owed him her life, as well as the lives of Tagar and Pika. Also, this would be the first night of Dakar's life away from home. They were lying right next to each other about eight feet into the den the pack used. It was on a hillside in a spruce thicket. The tunnel extended fifteen feet into the earth. Their chamber was in a fork off the main tunnel. Past their chamber was an enlarged chamber where the rest of the pack resided. There was no bedding used in the den. They could see anything approaching the den for a hundred feet from the entrance, which was about twenty-five inches in diameter.

"Torga, how long do you think it will take us to find Dakar?" Tanya asked apprehensively.

"I have no idea, since I don't know what his plan is, or where the humans are. Since they may still be stalking Dakar, we'll have to be careful we don't walk right into their trap. We're going to have to go slow, and we'll be staying off the trail he made. It's going to be slow and difficult." Torga spoke calmly, but he knew she would be able to see the worry in his eyes.

"Torga, I only have about a month before the babies will be here. We'll have to have a den soon. What will we do if we can't find Dakar before then?" Tanya's eyes were moist, and her intense soulful stare made Torga look away. He didn't want her to see his fears reflected in his eyes, and he knew she was always able to read his emotions.

"Let's not worry about something that may not happen. We may find Dakar right away. Don't worry, I'll take care of you," Torga said with forced confidence.

"But if we don't find him before we have to go to a den, it'll be a long time before we could look again. You'll have to help me feed the cubs, and it'll be weeks before we could even begin to look after that!" Desperation showed in her stare.

Torga put his paw protectively around Tanya's shoulder, and he licked her mouth and cheek lovingly as he said, "Tanya, I'll do everything I can to find Dakar. You know that. I can't endanger you or the pack, but I'll do what I can. That's all we can do. If he's all right, sooner or later either we'll find him or he'll find us. Let's get some rest now, because we're going to have a difficult journey starting tomorrow."

Tanya snuggled up next to Torga, putting her head right next to his. She closed her eyes, licked him reassuringly several times, then went to sleep.

*   *   *

The next morning the hunters arrived at the airport offices of John Sanders. Offices might be overstating the definition of the little corner of the old hanger where Sanders had an old metal desk and a much-used old wooden file cabinet. Sanders' friend, Josh Hankins, had let Sanders use this space in return for helping with the maintenance on the planes Hankins rented out.

Sanders saw the hunters enter the hanger opening and noticed that they already looked scruffy, even though it was only nine a.m. Sanders had learned shortly after meeting these two that it took them much of the morning to get over the hangovers from their nightly drinking binges. Winslow, the larger of the two, must have weighed three hundred pounds and little of it was muscle. His black floppy beard descended on his chest, thankfully covering his several drooping chins. Sanders knew these two had some money; they had paid for his services promptly so far, but they definitely didn't spend it on clothing. They both wore plaid shirts that had stains from several meals autographed on the sleeves, and their jeans looked like they had been used while their owners crawled through a muddy obstacle course.

Oh well, in this business one shouldn't expect to get the cream of society, Sanders thought. He knew his reputation as a guide that would cut corners and shave a few laws and regulations for the right price wasn't designed to appeal to the finer sides of human nature. However, the money was good, and he didn't much care where it came from.

"Looks like a decent day, John," Winslow said without conviction. "Do you think we'll be able to pick up the trail of that wolf? Ben and I want to have that trophy to spice up the tale we'll spin when we get back to Oklahoma. You'll have

57

more business than you can handle when our friends hear how you can find wolf packs. With all the hunters we'll send you from down home, there won't be any wolves left! Not even in the parks!" Winslow let out a wicked laugh, then started coughing uncontrollably for several minutes. He wiped his mouth on his shirtsleeve, then rubbed his sleeve on his jeans.

I don't know if even the amount I'm charging is worth dealing with more hunters like these two, Sanders though. "Well, boys, we'll do the best we can. The sky's clear, and we should be able to spot the tracks from the air. There are some towns and civilization in the direction that wolf was headed, though. We'll have to be careful. You boys wouldn't want to end up in a provincial jail, and neither would we."

Tunnell looked up. He was seated in a chair with his head flopping to the side, supported by his hand. "What, go to jail just for shooting a wolf? What idiot would do a thing like that to us?"

"If they find out we've been tracking them through the park, they sure might. I explained all that to you. You know the risks," Sanders replied.

Jacque, who had been resting on the wing of Sanders' plane while waiting, slowly lifted himself off the plane and joined the group. Jacque was rather small; 150 pounds and 5'9". He had been toughened, however, by eleven years in the federal prison system. He asked sarcastically, "Have you fellows taken the time this morning to practice your shooting? That would help next time you get the wolf in your sights."

"Look, Jacque, I would have nailed that durn wolf cold if my foot hadn't slipped on the ice," Winslow replied angrily.

"Calm down, calm down, Mon Cher. I was just making a joke. I *know* you would have, never fear." Jacque looked wryly at Sanders, who tried to look away but couldn't hold back a slight scornful smile. Sanders recovered by quickly saying, "Well, let's get cranked up, and we'll start looking for tracks by air, first. Finding a wolf that doesn't want to be found isn't easy, but 'ol Jacque here can track anything that touches the ground."

CHAPTER 7

Dakar looked at Rahwa with uneasiness. He realized that he had taken a lot for granted when he had allowed this raven to decide his course. He had just gone on instinct. Of course, his father had told him how valuable instinct could be to a wolf, but maybe he wasn't old or experienced enough. He stared intently into Rahwa's eyes, then said, "What is your trick? I can't afford to make any mistakes now. You can always just fly away, but I can't fly, and I can't run very well. I don't have a lot of choices."

Rahwa looked very unconcerned, despite Dakar's obvious anxiety, and said, "Here's the idea. When I saw the pack of wolves, I also saw a herd of deer just south of the pack in a clearing separated from the wolves by a stand of spruce trees. I just bet that if you went around so that the deer were between you and the wolves, they would rather have a good meal than run off one little bitty intruder. In addition, you have an advantage I'll bet a wolf would give up his den for, which is a pair of eyes, namely mine, up several hundred feet telling you where the deer are and where the wolves are. Now, how's that for an idea?"

Dakar was astounded. He thought of all the times Torga had used every bit of his knowledge and keen senses to try to feed his pack before they starved. He now realized what a difference it would make to have a pair of eyes up in the sky seeing everything. Maybe he had used good judgment, after all. Not wanting to admit he ever doubted Rahwa, he simply said, "Yeah, that might work. I guess we'll give it a try. Nothing to lose. Now, where do I go to get to the other side of the deer herd?"

Rahwa looked at Dakar, his eyes narrowing. "I suppose I'm going to have to wait for my thanks until you are out of the wolves' territory, since I'm obviously not going to get any now. Okay, here's what you do. Go down the trail to where you see that big tree sticking out next to the river. Then head east towards the mountains. That ought to get you on the other side of the deer. I'll get up in the sky to make sure. I'll meet up just after you head into the woods."

Having someone watching over me isn't such a bad thing. It's almost like having another father, Dakar thought. He realized he had a lot to learn, and in his world one mistake could cost him

Louis Dorfman

his life. He knew he was very lucky. Last summer a lone wolf had come into their territory, and even though his father had run him out, Tanya told him that he was probably orphaned by humans killing his family. She said she really felt sorry for him, but Torga couldn't afford to show any weakness, or the pack wouldn't respect him. He could now understand just how that lone wolf felt. He decided right then that if he lived through this and one day became the leader of the pack, he would find some way to show compassion for a lone wolf. Rahwa was right. Just because there were rules, they didn't have to always be blindly followed. There could be some exceptions.

Dakar realized he had better start focusing on his current problem. He had just reached the big Rocky Mountain maple that was his marker to turn east. He left the trail and walked slowly into the chest-deep snow under the spruce forest in front of him. The snow tickled his nose, but he knew not to make a sound, no matter what. The fresh smell of the pine needles from the lodgepole pine trees, mixed in with the spruce, reminded him of the area around his den, and he was suddenly very homesick. He had left scent-marks as often as he could, and that was all he could do about keeping a way open to return to the pack right now.

Rahwa suddenly appeared right in front of him. *Funny, I didn't see him flying down through the trees,* Dakar thought.

Rahwa grinned and said with satisfaction, "It looks like it's working perfectly. They are all where they're supposed to be. I'd suggest you go on over that ridge way up there in front. Then, I'll see where everyone is. If they're all in the right places, I'll signal you, and you make some kind of fuss that would make a wolf pack curious. They'll walk right into the deer herd. Careful, though, that you don't make too much fuss, or you'll scare the deer."

"You forget, I'm a wolf, too. I live by knowing how *not* to scare deer," Dakar said disgustedly.

"Yeah, well, I'm a perfectionist. When I have a plan, I don't want some macho wolf to mess it up by overplaying his hand. Just being sure. I'll whistle real loud when I see it's time for you to do whatever it is you do," Rahwa said, as he opened his wings, and fluttered a time or two, then ascended through the trees into the sky.

Funny, Dakar thought, *Rahwa's wings glowed just like they did this morning when I first saw him. But now, there's no sunlight. We're in the timber.*

Dakar went up to the ridge and lay down. The cold snow felt good against his shoulder, which was beginning to burn badly and hurt even worse. The whistling of the cool wind through the leaves made Dakar think about home and the comfort of his mother and the pack. He had spent many happy days on just such a ridge above their den listening to the leaves tinkle in the evening breeze.

In a few minutes he heard a whistle signal from Rahwa, and he looked up to be sure. After seeing Rahwa dip a wing in assurance, Dakar made a sound that was something between a whine and a bark. He knew it was a sound that would interest a wolf pack. He then crept through the pine trees until he spotted the deer. His sharp eyes spied the wolves on the other side of the deer; they had obviously seen the herd, and they were setting up a hunting pattern. Satisfied, he slowly slipped away and limped painfully down to the trail by the river. Now that the danger was lessened, his shoulder seemed to bother him more.

"Well, do I get any thanks for my plan, or not?" Rahwa said, as he appeared, seemingly out of nowhere.

"Yeah, you do. That was a good plan. You're okay, little bird. I wouldn't mind having you around all the time. I didn't realize how great it is to have someone up in the sky telling you what's going on below. It sure saves a lot of stalking and guesswork." Dakar grinned at Rahwa and attempted to lick him.

Rahwa flitted up to a tree branch, shaking his head. "Hey, go easy on the affection! I'm not one of your wolf pack! I *guess* that was an apology, which is accepted. Let's get on the road. We want to be out of their territory, 'cause I don't want to have to come up with another plan. Also, there's a humans' road that crosses our path several hours walk from here, and we want to cross it well before dark. I've seen a lot of creatures like you get blinded by the lights of the humans' machines after dark, and then they get hit."

Dakar's eyes narrowed to slits as he thought about humans and their machines. "I *hate* humans. I still don't know how a human is going to do anything for my shoulder when I can't stand to be around them. All I know about them is that they like to kill animals for pleasure."

"You're going to find that there are some good ones; the good ones are the ones that don't bother animals, so you've had no contact with them. They exist, though. Just trust me. You're going to like the ones I introduce you to. Believe me, it's going to have a big effect on your life and how you lead your pack. Humans don't have the strict rules you wolves live by. They are motivated by their individual rules, not the ones of a pack or a tradition. There are humans that have enough honor to sacrifice themselves for their family just like you were prepared to do, but those kind aren't going to come in the forest and bother you wolves."

"How do you know what I did for my family? I didn't tell you anything about it," Dakar asked. His eyes were wide open, and he looked completely confused.

Rahwa smiled sympathetically at Dakar's quizzical expression. "Oh, Dakar, you'll learn I know about things you couldn't possibly comprehend. Just accept it. I know all about you, and that's why I'm here."

Just at that moment, Dakar heard a slight crack and saw movement off to the left in the huckleberry bushes. He sniffed the air and picked up the unmistakable odor of a red squirrel. He dove headlong into the bushes purely on instinct. The tight bushes resisted his thrust and pulled against his shoulder, but he was still too quick for the unfortunate squirrel. He came out of the bush with his dinner. "I'll save some for you, little friend. We better eat when the food's available."

After the quick lunch, Rahwa said, "Dakar, we'd better get going. We want to cross that humans' trail with the hard surface well before dark."

"How long will it take for us to get to your Indian friend? I don't want to get so far from the pack that I'll never find them."

"We may be able to make it tomorrow. We *do* have to cross the mountain range over to the east, as I told you. I've never had to think about where to cross it on foot, but I think I know a place that won't be too bad for you."

Dakar didn't want to tell Rahwa how bad his shoulder hurt, but he could tell that it was getting worse. He felt hot, and his strength was waning. Dakar decided that this was one of the tests of a pack leader; he had to be able to endure pain, if necessary. *I'm not going to come this far and not make it to get help. Father told me sometimes you have to do things that you don't think you can do. I won't disappoint him,* Dakar thought.

Rahwa looked carefully at Dakar, silently nodded his head as if he were approving of something Dakar said, then flew up in the sky.

They continued on the trail for about thirty minutes. Then, Dakar started sniffing in a wide circle, which he made wider with each revolution. Finally satisfied, he called to Rahwa and said, "We are out of the pack's territory. We've passed that danger. I can *now* say thank you for getting me through it. I must admit, that was a good idea. This time of year, a wolf won't pass up the chance to get a deer, even for an intruder. They probably didn't even know I was there until after we were almost at the edge of their territory." Dakar lay down, relieved. The pain was worse than he thought he could endure.

"Oh, I've got better things in store for you, Dakar. Your life will never be the same. Just you wait and see," said Rahwa, and his eyes burned so brightly that Dakar had to look away from the intense gaze.

Dakar realized that after Rahwa stared at him, he somehow regained some of his energy. He got up and decided he could go on for a while longer. Rahwa flew up to his position above Dakar, and they proceeded down the trail.

Soon, Rahwa came down from the sky, and said, "Right up ahead through that line of trees is the humans' trail I told you about. They go up and down it in metal machines. I don't know if you have ever seen any of them, but they move much faster than you. You must look before you cross the trail. I didn't see any of them just now, but you never know. Be careful."

As Dakar nodded, Rahwa rose back into the sky. Dakar was watching Rahwa when Dakar saw movement out of the corner of his eye. He turned and there, coming out of the stand of fir trees, was a huge golden eagle. Dakar knew what it was; there were lots of them in the forests and mountains around Dakar's home. His father had told him to be careful around them; they had been known to carry off a small wolf cub. Dakar knew Rahwa would be easy prey for the eagle. He quickly let out a howl that he knew Rahwa would be able to hear. Rahwa looked and saw the eagle, which was bearing down on Rahwa with lightning speed. The eagle looked enormous with his light-colored head in contrast to his chocolate brown body. The eyes of the eagle were locked on his potential prey as he flew like a bullet directly at his target. Rahwa returned the stare with eyes that suddenly glowed like lasers, as he let out a curdling screech. Suddenly, the eyes of the eagle turned from that of a hunter to that of one facing sheer terror, and the eagle banked into a sharp turn and flew rapidly away, climbing as quickly as he could up to the clouds.

Dakar was stunned! He had known the eagle to be the most ferocious and fearless of all birds. He knew he was watching something well beyond his understanding. He also knew he might as well not ask what happened. Rahwa had already made it plain that he would explain whom or what he was when he was ready, if at all.

Rahwa didn't even bother to come down out of the sky, so Dakar continued through a fir thicket and found himself at a cleared area on which was a paved road. Dakar had seen some of these roads the previous summer around the wolf pack's home area so he wasn't totally unfamiliar with them. He knew about the strange machines that used these paths, and he looked carefully before dashing across.

Dakar's shoulder was beginning to hurt very badly again after the quick sprint across the road, and he saw that in front of them was a formidable range of mountains. As soon as he reached the security of the spruce forest in front of him, he let out a whimpering bark, which got Rahwa's attention.

As soon as Rahwa descended, Dakar said, "My shoulder feels really bad. I just can't go any further right now. I must rest for a while. Do you think we can stop for the night somewhere near here?"

Rahwa smiled with pride, saying, "You're in luck. There just happens to be a tree up on the hill just ahead called an alpine fir. Its gum is a great antiseptic, and antiseptic is something that will help your shoulder until we get to my Indian friend. Also, there's a place near the fir trees that would make a great temporary den for the night. We'll just stay there." Rahwa then led Dakar carefully up the mountain to the clump of fir trees.

"Now, Rahwa, how will we get this stuff you called gum out of these trees?" asked Dakar curiously.

"Oh, that's the most interesting part. I have a friend that lives near here, and it'll be a snap for him to get all the gum you need for your shoulder."

"Oh, great," mumbled Dakar glumly, "so now there's another human involved that you didn't tell me about."

"Goodness, no!" said Rahwa indignantly. "My friend, Sulman, is no human. He's a grizzly bear!"

What have I gotten myself into? Dakar thought. *All I knew before was my pack and our territory. All these new things coming at once are more than I can begin to understand. What does this raven have in store for me, I wonder?*

71

CHAPTER 8

Torga got the pack up at the first light of day. He had slept badly; he was worried about Dakar on the cub's first night away from his family. He also knew they would have to travel slowly on their search and watch out for danger at every turn. Not only would they be going into strange country, but also they would be following Dakar, who might have the hunters on his trail. The familiar scent of the den the pack had used for several years penetrated the early still morning. The sun beginning to filter through the limbs of the trees around the den made Torga long for the lazy days of summer soon to come. He knew the next days would be difficult and dangerous. He nuzzled Tanya, who had lain back down and gone to sleep. He knew the additional burden of a litter of cubs growing inside her sapped her energy.

"Tanya, we must go," Torga gently growled. "We'll need every bit of daylight available. We can't stay right on Dakar's trail; it's too risky. We're going to have to make our own path through the forest."

Tanya stretched, yawned, then said, "I'm sorry. You're right. We've got to get going. Besides, we're going to have much more trouble than Dakar getting food. After all, we've got to feed a whole pack, and, of course, a bunch of babies," she said with a grin.

Tanya went outside the den where the rest of the pack was waiting. "Maya, you, Surle, and Halwa are going to be in charge of the cubs. During this trip, I'm going to be up front with Torga. The cubs aren't to be allowed any playing while we're on the trail. It's going to be dangerous."

Tagar and Pika, apparently upset that they weren't being treated as full members of the pack, started wrestling with their aunts. They pushed Maya, the oldest of the females, onto her side and ganged up on her, nipping at her throat and her legs.

Torga, hearing the brawl, came out to see what was going on. He didn't want anything to distract from the search. He immediately jumped into the fray with jaws slashing. He grabbed Tagar by the nose and flipped him onto his back. He then wrapped his jaws tightly around Tagar's neck until all four of Tagar's legs were extended in submission. Then, before Pika could plead for mercy, he knocked her on her side, grabbed one of her forelegs, and rolled her onto her back. He then duplicated the action he had taken with Tagar until Pika likewise indicated complete submission.

"Now, you both have shown you're not entitled to be treated like adults," Torga growled menacingly. "When there is a dangerous job to do, you are *never* to waste any energy on any unnecessary activity. Is that *clear*?"

With head and tail held low, Tagar replied, "Yes, father. You are right. We're sorry. It won't happen again."

Pika, her head even lower than her brother's, nodded assurance, saying, "We just got carried away. We won't do it again. We're worried about Dakar, too."

Tanya, watching Torga give a strong lesson in discipline, just ignored her cubs while Torga disciplined them. Then she said, "Don't forget, if Dakar hadn't risked his life for you, you wouldn't be here today."

Tagar and Pika hung their heads and tails in submission and shame. "Yes, mother!" they said in unison.

Torga took the pack to the spot where Dakar had entered the timber. He could still easily smell Dakar's scent. The scent would be readable under most conditions for about three days. In addition, it had not snowed, so the prints were still visible in most places. They followed the trail, keeping a constant vigil for any signs of humans in the area. Torga snarled as he detected the pursuing hunters' footsteps following Dakar.

As the trail took them towards the pass Dakar had crossed, Torga had a satisfied feeling of pride, for he knew what Dakar was doing. Tanya saw Torga's change of expression, and in answer to her quizzical look, said, "I know this area. Our son is leading the humans away from our home and then over a mountain pass. He'll probably go across a river that is below the pass. We raised him well!" Torga's chest swelled with pride, and he knew he had to find Dakar, no matter what it took. In addition to his personal love for his son, it was for the good of the pack.

Tanya smiled with understanding, saying, "We do raise great cubs, don't we? If we have another litter as good as the last, we'll have the best pack in the land. Oh, Torga, we've just got to find him!"

The melodic sounds of the warblers and the thrushes in the fir trees along their route were a stark contrast to the silent, determined attitude of the pack. The wolves were now totally focused.

Torga gathered the pack in a semi-circle, then said, "I want you questioning any sound you hear that isn't in rhythm with the normal noises of the forest. A mistake in this unfamiliar territory might cost us our lives."

The pack each silently nodded acceptance. They realized they would not know where to seek safety, as they would in their own surroundings. Torga then nodded, turned, and led the way alongside Dakar's tracks.

Torga noticed the fresh smell of the sap starting to rise in the evergreens, and together with the warm feel of the morning sun, it was apparent that spring was near at hand.

That also means a new litter of cubs to care for. Dakar would be the one binding the pack together when I'm busy caring for the family and seeking extra food to regurgitate for the new cubs, he thought. *There are many reasons this search must be successful.*

They reached the top of Sinclair Pass well before noon, and Torga could sense the scene that had taken place there as soon as they descended towards the river.

Torga turned to Tanya and said grimly, "Right here is where that metal bird set down. I can smell the excitement of the humans and their thirst for Dakar's blood. All four of the hunters' tracks are present here. They must have been close to Dakar, judging by the way they were carelessly running around."

Tanya's heart was beating so fast Torga could hear it, and his feelings went out to her. While he hated to show his feelings for her in front of the others, he gently licked her face, her mouth, and her cheeks while placing his paw tenderly on her shoulder. He then rubbed his body alongside hers, pushing into her sides while rubbing his head next to hers. Tanya responded with a series of whimpers, and even Tagar and Pika were silent with their heads hanging down in a submissive and respectful posture. Maya, Halwa, and Surle were quietly whining in sympathy, while Mutar kept a silent and vigilant watch on the surrounding countryside.

Torga appreciated Mutar's loyalty and his capability to be satisfied and secure with his subordinate, but important, position in the pack. Torga could always count on Mutar to do the right thing when it was necessary for the safety or needs of the pack. He was a good soldier, and Torga would always protect him with his life.

"Tanya, it's a good sign that there are no vultures anywhere in the sky. On a clear, sunny day like today they would quickly find any large dead body. Dakar is very smart and very strong. I'm sure he can outwit those humans. Let's go check the river," Torga said with forced optimism.

As soon as Torga crossed the river he smelled Dakar's tracks; unfortunately his joy was tempered by the sight and smell of blood along Dakar's trail.

"Tanya," he said as she rushed over to him, "he's all right. He's been hurt but not severely. See, there's not too much blood, and his gait is strong and steady. Look, he rested over here then began heading south. He's obviously leading those hunters away from us. We've got to be very careful or we might run into the hunters if they're following Dakar. We're going to have to take a path in the woods parallel to his trail. In the open we'd be easy to see in that metal bird the humans use. We can't expect to catch up with him quickly. With the pack, we're going to have to find more food than Dakar needs. It's going to take longer."

"Of course, you're right. I'm so worried about him, though. I wonder how he got hurt. Do you think it was one of those metal sticks with the loud noise? He must be so scared and lonely, all alone in a strange territory. He's never been without his family! Oh, please, let's find him as soon as we possibly can. He's never even had to feed himself! Torga, for all his bravery, he's still a cub," Tanya said, whimpering quietly as she spoke.

Torga had to turn away. He couldn't stand to see Tanya so unhappy. "I know, but it won't do any good to break pack security and go off recklessly. We'd only get hurt, and it wouldn't help Dakar. We'll do it right, but we'll find him. If we can't get to him before we have to build a den for the new cubs, I'll send Mutar and Maya after him. They're dependable. Halwa and Surle should be able to handle Pika and Tagar." Torga cast a warning glance at the cubs as he spoke, and the cubs responded by sinking their heads and their tails very low, almost to the ground.

Torga started examining Dakar's tracks again. "Humm, this is interesting. It doesn't appear that the hunters crossed the river. I can't find their scent or footsteps anywhere. We have to assume they are still after Dakar, but they must be in that metal bird."

Torga led the pack along Dakar's route, mostly keeping off the trail. They walked carefully through the melting snow, but the crunching sound their footsteps made in the snow sounded like trees falling to the vigilant Torga. In early afternoon, they found the spot where Dakar had spent his first night, and Torga's ears quickly pointed up, as did his tail. He bared his teeth with the corners of his mouth pulled forward.

79

"What's wrong, Torga?" asked Tanya. "I don't see or hear anything."

"I can sense that Dakar had an encounter with something here that's very strange. Whoever, or whatever, it is gives off a scent that I remember once smelling when I was a cub. There is the odor of a bird, but not quite. It is much too strong, and the intensity of it would make me think it would be much larger than any bird I've ever seen. I don't sense that it was necessarily a threat to Dakar, though. It's just unlike anything I know. I feel that Dakar was comfortable with it, and that bothers me. He's just not old enough to know how to deal with something new to him. He's liable to trust too much."

"Well, I trust Dakar's judgment. Look how he saved the cubs and me. And, look how he led those awful humans away from us. You just don't want to recognize that he's going to be a grown wolf before you know it," Tanya said defensively.

As Torga was about to respond, Mutar arrived. He had been out on the eastern flank keeping watch for any potential danger.

"Torga, I thought I'd better let you know. There's a group of moose just over the hill in a willow grove, and I didn't think you'd want to let a good meal go by. Who knows when we'll find food again in this unfamiliar territory?" Mutar asked matter-of-factly.

Torga nodded appreciatively. "Yes, we want to take advantage of any good opportunities to eat. I don't think this journey is going to be short, and we have to eat at every chance, especially Tanya," Torga said, as he glanced at Tanya with a smile.

*   *   *

The hunters were airborne, and it was apparent that the flight was not easy for Tunnell. His face had turned from a ruddy red to a pasty white, and his red eyes were bulging with the obvious effort to keep his breakfast down. "Do you think we'll be landing soon?" he asked hopefully.

"Well, I could land, but I don't have any idea at all where the wolf is now," Sanders answered. "If you wanted to be on land, you shouldn't have come to start with." Sanders was disgusted with the fact that fate had dictated that he be dependant on slobs like Tunnell. He had once been a proud member of the Canadian Mounted Police, but getting caught poaching bear several years ago had cost him that career. He cursed the fact that a greedy woman had made him do something he didn't really want to do just so he could earn easy money. That time, a tourist from Japan had offered him $10,000 for a grizzly bear. Something about some crazy notion that the glands of the bear would cure some disease he had. The money had just been too tempting. *Now, look what it cost me*, he thought. *My constant companion is Jacque, an ex-con of the sort I would have enjoyed putting back in the slammer several years ago. Now, because Jacque is such a good tracker, he's a partner. It's all the fault of those durn wild animals everyone wants to kill.* He *still* had Stacy, but she did need a lot of money. He knew he would only have her as long as he could afford her, though, so that led him back to the Tunnells of the world.

"I'll tell you what. We'll set down at Canal Flats. That's about thirty miles south of where we last saw that wolf. Then we'll head over towards the river and see what we can find. I know someone in Canal Flats whose jeep I can probably borrow."

Tunnell sighed with relief. "I'll try to hold out till then, but I hope it's close."

Sanders set the plane down in a small meadow about a half-mile east of the small town. His friend lived on a farm not far from the meadow. The melting snow was a little tricky for the plane, but Sanders was a good pilot, whatever else he was.

As soon as Tunnell departed the plane, he could wait no longer and lost his breakfast. *That's just like the way the day began,* Sanders thought. *This might be one of those ventures that are hexed from the beginning; however, these men do have the money, and they pay well.*

The group waited by the plane while Sanders went to his friend's farm. He returned about an hour later with a five year old jeep with most of the paint peeled off, but it had good snow tires and a winch in case they got stuck.

They headed down a little trail to a spot where the White River and the Lussier River forked.

"My guess is the wolf probably used a trail that was right at the spot where we last saw him on the east side of the Kootenay River," Jacque said. "That is, if he keeps going south. If he continued down that trail he would end up somewhere near this crossing. If not, then we'll have to start back where we last saw him."

The trail was narrow, and it wound through a fir grove towards the river. The grove was thick, and Sanders had to keep his attention on the imperceptible trail. The slushy snow kept tugging at the wheels of the jeep, making the thought of getting stuck a very likely possibility. Soon they reached the fork of the two rivers. Jacque presumed that the wolf, if he continued south, would cross the river not far from the fork. There was a narrow section at that location where most of the river was frozen over.

Once they reached the fork, Jacque got out and started walking along the Lussier River to the east. He was carefully checking the snow at each step, and he had told the rest of the group to stay far back so that nothing would be disturbed. That was completely satisfactory to Tunnell and Winslow. They wanted in on the kill, but they had no love for the details of the search.

"I thought you said this was going to be an easy kill," Winslow complained as he rubbed his back.

Sanders jumped up off the tree stump he was using for a chair, started towards Winslow, then stopped himself, and said furiously, "You had your shot at an easy kill yesterday. If you want anything easier than that, you're going to have to go to a zoo."

Tunnell stepped between them. "Calm down, fellows. You both have your points, but the main thing is we've got to get this wolf. We sure aren't going to leave here while he's getting the best of us, now are we, Henry?"

Winslow was obviously taken back by Sanders' reaction. "All right, all right. Sorry. We aren't going home without him now, that's for sure."

Jacque stopped and started looking carefully at the ground. "Here!" he called out loudly. "I've found our wolf!"

The group plodded over, and Jacque showed them the paw prints in the snow.

"I'd say, by the amount of melting snow around the prints, that it has been at least several hours since he was here. John, there is something strange about this. I've never seen a wolf make a trail so easy to find. This wolf doesn't act like he's very smart, but his actions yesterday contradict that."

"Do you think he may be laying an obvious trail, then circling back? I've heard of wolves doing that," Sanders said thoughtfully.

"That's very possible. The forests south of here are pretty thick, so it'd be difficult to drive along the trail further south. It's probably wiser to get back in the plane and see what we can find that way."

"Okay, and we'll look back up north a ways. He might have doubled back. I sure don't want to be outsmarted by a wolf!"

Louis Dorfman

It's bad enough, I've got to do this, just so I can keep Stacy happy, he thought. *Sure don't want some critter I don't care anything about getting the best of me, too.*

CHAPTER 9

"You mean you're going to get a grizzly bear to come get some sap out of these fir trees to help my shoulder? He's just going to come here and help me? Don't you know that bears and wolves compete for food? They wouldn't particularly want to help a competitor, even if they *are* good and kind animals!" Dakar growled.

"Now, Dakar," Rahwa said patiently, "haven't I done all right by you so far? You're going to have to learn to trust me, my friend. Just wait here—I'll be back soon. I know where Sulman and his mate live. They just woke up from their winter sleep not too many days ago, and they have a little cub that you'll just love. Trust me!" Rahwa rose up into the sky in a blur, and Dakar was left to wonder if he should continue to blindly follow him.

Soon Rahwa reappeared, and again Dakar did not see or hear his approach. Dakar was becoming annoyed at the ease with which Rahwa could appear so suddenly.

"I found them, and they are more than happy to help. Don't worry, they are two of the gentlest creatures around here. Just be careful with their baby. They're kinda sensitive about her. This is Mada's first cub," Rahwa said.

"Great! Now, as hurt and sore as I am, I've got to worry about getting on the wrong side of a bear cub," Dakar said testily. It was becoming evident that Dakar's shoulder was much worse than he wanted to admit, and Rahwa observed him closely, worried that he wouldn't make it much further.

"When we get to the Indian's home and Kattana gets hold of you, you'll feel much better, don't worry," Rahwa said gently. "What we're going to do now is just patch you up temporarily until I can get you there."

Soon they heard a rumble that sounded like a small avalanche thundering through the tangle of ferns, white rhododendrons, and black huckleberry bushes that formed a thick undergrowth beneath the fir trees. The sight and sounds of the bushes shaking and the snow falling off the tops of the trees as they were pushed aside was unsettling. Dakar could feel the ground shaking as he heard the splat of huge feet resounding off the soft snow.

"Well, where's our little injured wolf?" boomed a deep voice, as the light was eclipsed by the largest animal Dakar had ever seen. Dakar had to stretch his neck to see the face of the huge creature standing upright. The smell of the giant's fur was musky and strong, emphasizing his massive proportions. Dakar didn't know whether to speak, run, or just stand there staring.

"Hello, little fellow," Sulman said. "I hear you're another victim of the human's sport, as they call it. I can't imagine it being fun to kill when you don't need to, but then we'll never understand humans, right?"

The friendliness and warmth of the giant bear made Dakar start to relax, and he said, "I'm not even a year old, so I haven't had much experience with humans. I *hate* them, though. We were a happy pack, not bothering them, and they dropped in with this metal bird and started trying to kill my family. I'm now trying to lead them away from my pack."

"Yeah, Rahwa told me you're a hero. He said they got you with those metal rods that throw a piece of metal. Some of that alpine fir gum will fix you up until Rahwa gets you to Kattana." As Sulman was talking, the rumbling began again signaling the entrance of Mada, his mate. She broke through the undergrowth with a bound and stopped just short of Dakar.

Dakar shuddered at the sight of these two mammoth creatures obliterating the light and looming over him like a furry mountain. Dakar was speechless, and he couldn't believe he was feeling comfortable with someone who could kill him with one swipe of a paw.

"Goodness me," Mada said. "So this cute little wolf is the one that made fools of those humans! I'm sure glad to meet you and more glad we could help. Sulman, don't just stand there looking! Get some of that gum and let's get this deserving little fellow feeling better. I heard you protected your family. That's good enough for me. Oh, this little baby behind me is kinda shy. Her name is Meyote."

Dakar saw a curious, mischievous face peeking out from behind Mada. While Meyote was a baby, she weighed almost as much as Dakar. She had a sweet, angelic face that reminded him of his beloved sister, Miya, and a grin that let him know she was as playful as she was sweet. He finally collected himself, and said, "My name's Dakar. I can't believe you are helping me, but I really thank you. My father *did* tell me that grizzly bears are kind, and he told me a story about how one time a bear like you let him eat some of his food when things were bad."

"Yes, well, with humans taking over most of the property and driving animals like you and us off our family lands, we have to stick together," Sulman said. "That's why Rahwa is taking you to Kattana. You said you hate humans, but Indians have as much reason to hate the white-faced humans as we do. The white-faced humans drove the Indians off their families' lands just like they're doing to us. You can't hate everyone just because they are a human. There are good ones, too. I bet there's even a bad wolf or two lurking around somewhere." Sulman's eyes twinkled, and Dakar felt much more relaxed with him.

Mada looked at Sulman with a piercing stare, saying, "I want you to get that gum for his shoulder *now*! We don't want to wait 'till he's an old fellow before we heal him." Dakar couldn't believe such a ferocious-looking creature could look so sheepish as Sulman strode over to the alpine fir tree and, with one massive slash, opened up the bark and dug into the pulp of the tree about four inches. Sulman then dug out some of the gum and brought it over to Dakar. Rahwa was standing next to Dakar's shoulder, and he was obviously enjoying the interchange between the wolf and the bears. He had a prankish expression on his face, as if he had created a great play and he was observing the results of it. As Sulman brought over the gum, Rahwa said, "Put it on the sore flesh there on his shoulder. Be careful, because those claws of yours could really hurt." As Sulman gently placed the gum on the wound, Rahwa rubbed it into the flesh with his beak until the wound was completely covered.

I can't believe this is happening, Dakar thought. *Here's a bear putting medicine on me, and a bird rubbing it in. I hope I'm using good judgment. So far it's worked out okay.*

Meyote soon lost her shyness, and she puffed up her lips in a pout as she saw that someone other than she was getting all the attention. She bounced across the snow right into the middle of the circle, knocking Dakar off his feet and rolling across him into a ball on the other side.

"Meyote! Mind your manners!" Mada said without conviction. It was apparent that Mada was spoiling her first child. Meyote got the sweet, innocent expression of a fine teddy bear on her face and, with a smile, bounced right back into Dakar.

Dakar was in no condition to play. However, Meyote reminded him so much of Miya that he had to try. He pushed snow into Meyote's face with his nose and went behind the cub, kicking snow onto the cub's back with his hind feet. Meyote was happy to have a playmate her own size. She reached for Dakar with her paw, but Dakar anticipated her move. Dakar avoided the awkward cub and pushed against Meyote until she rolled in the snow. Alarmed at first by Dakar's actions, the adult bears soon relaxed and let the two cubs harmlessly tussle. They saw that Dakar was much more athletic, but he was being extremely gentle.

"My word, I believe we could get used to having Dakar around," Mada said to Sulman. "See, I told you Meyote needs a playmate. Let's see if we can't talk him and Rahwa into staying a while."

Rahwa, who had been silent throughout the exchanges, said with sorrow, "Unfortunately, we can't. We have a mission to fulfill. Also, I want Kattana to take care of that shoulder as soon as possible. Dakar's trying to show he's a tough wolf and all, but he's in worse shape than he's letting on. That shoulder's infected and needs more help than we can give him. We could stay tonight, though. I imagine Dakar would appreciate a warm bed and the security of being with you for the night. Then, he could at least get a good night's sleep."

Dakar, who had for the moment forgotten his journey and his lonesomeness, stopped playing when he heard Rahwa. "Would you let us stay with you in your den? I've heard how terrific a bear's den is. I thought it would be a long time before I saw *any* den again."

Meyote, who hadn't yet learned to talk, smiled and pulled on Dakar's neck with her paw. When Dakar let the cub pull him close, Meyote put both paws around his neck and used her six-inch tongue to give him a wet bear kiss that started at his chin and went over his ears.

"Here's the way we do it, Meyote," Dakar said, as he used the mouth-licking action wolves bestow on their families. Rahwa had a look of total satisfaction as he grinned from ear to ear.

Sulman smiled at the friendship the cub and wolf were sharing. "Oh, by the way, there are some marmots and ptarmigan around our den, in case you're hungry," he said. "We normally eat berries, but if you make a kill and don't want it all, we'll take the rest."

"I don't know if I'm capable of doing any hunting right now. My shoulder *is* hurting pretty bad. I'll see how it feels after I've had a chance to rest," Dakar responded. Dakar was delighted to have his new friends. This was the first time he had felt at ease since he had left his pack and family. He knew he was safe for now from everything except the dreaded humans. *I can see how nice it is when different animals work together and help each other. I won't forget this lesson,* Dakar thought.

Rahwa smiled at Dakar and nodded, as if he had read his mind. "I bet you'll feel much better after you've rested. The gum will help your wound temporarily, you'll see. Let's go to the den, and you'll have time to rest up and still hunt before dark."

Sulman led the group up the mountain to a spot hidden in a dense undergrowth of vines. During the trip up, Meyote delighted in pawing at Dakar's tail, keeping it up until she got a response from her new playmate. Dakar then would kick snow with his hind legs, throwing snow in Meyote's face. Meyote would giggle like a little baby and roll around, then jump up and repeat the process. Dakar growled unconvincingly as his mouth curled up in a smile. Mada looked on approvingly, happy to see her cub having such a good time with her new friend.

Soon they entered an opening barely large enough for the huge bears to squeeze through, but inside it opened into a large chamber that was quite comfortable for the group.

This is so much like my life was at home, he thought, as he lay down and put his head on his paws. *I had such a wonderful, carefree life. It's gone all because of those terrible humans!*

His eyes drooped, and the family of bears silently looked down at him. Mada imperceptibly motioned to Meyote, who giggled and flopped right on top of Dakar, tugging at Dakar's tail while licking the wolf's face with her damp tongue. The little bear rolled over on her back with all four feet sticking straight up in the air. To Dakar this was a sign of submission. However, when Dakar stood over Meyote in the classic wolf pose signifying dominance, he quickly found out that to a bear this was definitely not submission. Meyote started pawing at Dakar's neck and lapping his nose with her huge wet tongue. Dakar licked the little cub's belly, eliciting little giggles of joy. Dakar realized that his new friend was not going to let him dwell on his loneliness and thoughts of his family. While the smells in the bear den were strange to him, the feelings of friendship and love he felt flowing from the bears made it seem like home.

Dakar lay down again, but this time with a smile, and said, "Thank you all so much for making me feel at home. This is the first time since I left my family I haven't been scared and alone. I'll never forget your kindness. If it's okay, I'd like to sleep for a while now."

Mada softly said, "Go to sleep. You're completely safe while you're here. I'll keep little Meyote from bothering you while you rest." Meyote, understanding her mother, lay down by Dakar and gently stroked his back with her claws until he went fast asleep.

Rahwa watched the tender scene with obvious satisfaction. He whispered, "I really don't like being enclosed like this, and I can see you have Dakar very comfortable. I think I'll just go outside and make sure everything is okay. I'll see you when Dakar wakes up."

CHAPTER 10

Torga led his pack over the hill very quietly and carefully. He turned around and signaled to Mutar. "Make sure everyone stays silent. We can't use any more effort than necessary on this hunt. We have to keep our strength. We don't know what we may run into here in strange territory." Mutar nodded his understanding.

I can't believe it has only been one day since Dakar left, Torga thought. *There may be a long search ahead of us. We can't pass up a chance like this to get food, but I have to watch Tanya carefully; she's not going to tell me if she's getting tired. She wants to find Dakar so very much; so do I.*

He looked carefully through the tangle of buffalo berries at the top of the hill and saw six grown moose and three calves eating in a willow grove about one hundred yards away. He lay down quietly, made sure the rest of the pack lay very still behind him, and watched the movements of the herd for about ten minutes.

He noticed that one of the moose was very old and didn't seem to walk as well as the others, and he decided that one would be their target. He knew that if they were successful, they could go several days without eating without endangering Tanya's health. She had eaten a good meal the day before, and she would be adequately nourished for quite a while with one more good meal. He felt they had to seize this opportunity. He checked the wind direction and satisfied himself that the wind was blowing into their faces, not allowing their scent to drift to the moose. He then crept stealthily back, making sure not to disturb the berry bush or shake any leaves.

"Tanya, we'll use the same attack pattern as before. This time, though, I don't want you running the herd. You've got a hard trip ahead of you. When you get close enough, let Maya lead the charge. Mutar and I will be waiting to the south, as always," Torga said quietly.

"Okay. It'll take us longer to get in position than it will you, so we'll just start when the time is right."

Tanya led the pack around through the pine forest. She didn't say anything to the cubs, apparently satisfied that the lecture their father had given them earlier would keep them in line. They took about an hour to get properly in position. As soon as she decided that they had gotten as close as they could without prematurely alarming the moose, she nodded to Maya.

Maya had been with the pack for four years, and she was experienced and dependable. She led the charge as the pack burst out of the timber with snow flying in all directions. The moose panicked, as the wolves expected. The moose ran in the opposite direction from the charging wolves, right into Torga's position.

Torga had to use a different technique this time, for a moose is larger than a caribou. When the older moose was in the right position, Torga charged from his hiding place with blinding speed and power. He hurled himself right at the moose's shoulder with such force that the moose lost his balance. Mutar was charging at the moose's hind legs, knowing precisely what Torga was going to do. When the moose lost his balance, Mutar was there to pull the moose down by one of his hind legs. Before the moose could get back up, the remainder of the pack was there to help finish the attack.

"Great work, all of you," Torga stated through gulps of breath. He knew that it was rare for any pack to be successful twice in a row at a kill. Most of the time, they were lucky to make one kill in five tries. He realized the pack knew the importance of this journey, and he wanted them to know he appreciated their dedication. He even gave a smile to Tagar and Pika. The cubs were so delighted that they danced around and licked first his mouth, then Tanya's, with sincere delight. They even made sure to lick the aunts and their uncle. The pack would not have to worry about food for some time to come. Torga began eating his meal first, followed in precise order by Tanya, Mutar, Maya, Halwa, and Surle. The cubs did not try to get ahead their turn this time. Torga was very pleased, for now the pack could search for Dakar without having to worry about food for several days. He would have liked to stay at this location for an extra day and finish the moose, but he knew that Tanya would be upset if they didn't immediately continue on the journey to find Dakar. He saw her looking inquiringly at him, and said, "I know what you're thinking. We'll go on searching. I hate to leave food to waste, but I know how you feel. I'm anxious to find our son, too."

Tanya's eyes softened, and she smiled as she said, "Thank you. Don't worry about me. I'll be fine. I don't need to be babied as much as you think. I feel all right, and with this meal I can go a long time before I need more food. I would never get over it if anything happened to Dakar because we weren't there in time. There's just so much Dakar doesn't know about the world; I don't know how he's going to get by without us."

"Tanya, you're going to feel that way about each one of our cubs when the time comes to let them go; I agree the time is not yet here for Dakar, though. He shouldn't be making decisions on his own for another year or so." Torga was about to say something more when he heard the dreaded sound of the metal bird. His ears stood erect, and he concentrated all his senses on deciphering the location and direction of the sound.

"Quick, forget eating! Head for the forest! The humans are coming back!" Torga growled, as he leap towards the closest stand of timber about twenty yards away. The pack moved with military precision; they had often had to act in concert to survive. They were tightly huddled, so that there were no laggards falling behind when they entered the safety of the thick pine forest. Torga led them to some thick bushes, and they lay down in the thickest part. "Hold very still until I say otherwise!" Torga commanded.

*   *   *

Sanders and his group had begun the search for Dakar from the plane again. He first flew past the location where they found that Dakar had crossed the river, but about thirty miles south of there the tracks faded away.

"That is one smart wolf," Jacque said respectfully. "I really wouldn't be surprised if he backtracked along his own tracks, or went into the woods and then backtracked to his home territory."

"Well," Sanders said, "let's just backtrack ourselves and see what we can find. We've got plenty of daylight, and we can cover a lot of territory in this clear weather." He then banked the plane and headed north along the path next to the river. They could see the tracks plainly in several places.

They had gone about thirty minutes, when Jacque shouted, "I see something over that hill to the right! It looks like a carcass."

Sanders sharply banked the plane, and they headed in the direction Jacque indicated. In no time, they were over the moose lying in the open meadow.

"It looks like a moose, most likely killed by some wolves," Jacque stated. "But, I don't see any wolves around. Without checking it out on the ground, I wouldn't know how old it is. It hasn't decomposed, so it isn't too old."

"Do you think it could be our wolf?" asked Tunnell hopefully.

"Oh, no." said Jacque. "It would take a lot of strong wolves to get a moose as big as that one down. That size moose could kill one wolf pretty easy. Especially, one no bigger than the one we're after."

"Jacque, do you think it could be the rest of the pack from yesterday?" Sanders asked excitedly. "Maybe we can take out our revenge on the whole bunch after all, then junior would be without a pack. That'd give us our revenge on him. Now we're talking!"

"Well, Mon Cher, I don't think that pack would be anywhere around here. I've been watching their territory for several months, and I know it doesn't go anywhere near here. Wolves usually stay in their own territory, and besides, when they took off yesterday they headed the other direction. I doubt they would backtrack and come all the way over here, just because one of the pack is gone. No, I think this is another pack, and it's just a coincidence. It does tell me that *our* wolf wouldn't backtrack through here, though. If he once made it through another pack's territory, he wouldn't try it again so soon. They'd be watching, for sure!" Jacque answered confidently.

Sanders listened to Jacque's explanation with annoyance. He trusted Tremaine's judgment, but he didn't like what he was hearing. "Okay, I know you know wolves. I sure would like to get my hands on that pack, though. Let's head back south and see if we can't pick up the trail below that river crossing."

"Look, I thought we were going to go get that wolf today, not fly around the Canadian countryside looking at dead moose," Winslow complained. "If we have to track him on foot, let's do so. We're not paying this kind of money for a sightseeing tour."

Sanders looked at Winslow with a sneer, saying, "I was trying to make it easy on you two. You didn't look like you could make it very far from the plane this morning, but if it's tracking you want, it's tracking you're going to get. I'll just find the last place we can see any of his tracks, and then we'll go get him. But, don't say you're getting tired and want to quit, once we start." Tunnell looked at his partner with something between disgust and fear, but he didn't say a word.

They flew around the trails leading from the last sighting of tracks south of Lussier river in ever-wider circles, and finally Jacque motioned to fly lower just north of Highway 3. After they got about 100 feet above the ground, Jacque shouted, "There! Just north of the road, see the tracks moving in a semi-circle. It looks like he was looking at something, or he was trying to decide where to go. See! The tracks then appear on the other side of the highway. We've found our wolf! Look, right after he crossed the road, he started climbing up the mountain. There must be something up there that got his attention. I'll bet if we find a landing place somewhere near the top, we can backtrack down towards his tracks and pick them up without having to climb all the way up from the highway."

"That sounds like the best plan I've heard today," Winslow said with relief. "My vote and my money say let's do just that. How about you, Ben?"

"I like the idea of walking down the mountain a lot better than walking up. Let's do it. What have we got to lose? We could never walk up as fast as a wolf."

Sanders said nothing, but turned his plane east towards the MacDonald Range of mountains started climbing. *I really wish that had been the kill of the rest of the pack,* he thought. *I would love to have another go at bagging the lot of them.*

CHAPTER 11

Dakar awoke after sleeping just over an hour. He had slept deeply knowing he was safe for the first time since he had left his family. He had slipped into consciousness once during his sleep after dreaming he was home in his den. He had then felt the warm soft fur of Meyote next to him and realized he had thought it was his mother in his sleep. Now that he was awake, he still was happy that the little bear cub had cuddled up beside him; Meyote so reminded him of his little sister, Miya, who had died during the winter. He rolled over so that he was facing Meyote and slowly licked the little cub's cheeks. The cub started making small whimpering growls, and her lips curled back in a delightful smile. Suddenly, her eyes popped open, and she grabbed the startled wolf around the neck, licking his face like an ice cream cone.

Mada looked over at the two playful cubs. She was happy to see her little baby having so much fun with another child. She asked, "How's the shoulder, Dakar?"

Dakar had not thought about his wound until that moment. He attempted to stretch his leg. "It's still stiff, but it doesn't

107

seem to hurt as badly. I think that medicine helped some. I wonder if I really need to see that human friend of Rahwa's."

"Trust Rahwa, Dakar. We've known him for some time. He's special. The things he does are beyond my understanding, but he only wants to do things to help us animals. I've seen him help quite a few over the years. He seems to just appear when someone is worthy of help, and then he's gone again. He stops by here every so often, and we do what we can to help. One of Sulman's cousins was caught in a metal jaw tied to a tree a few years ago. It was put there by some humans. Rahwa just appeared, and even though we bears couldn't open the jaws, Rahwa just touched it and it opened. He does miraculous things when he's around. He obviously thinks you're special. He doesn't feel that way often. I know you'll be glad you met him, believe me."

Dakar was silent for some time. He was being asked to grow up very quickly. He had just been a wolf cub in a happy pack with loving parents one day ago. Now he was in strange country with a family of bears talking about a mysterious raven that he was being asked to follow on faith alone. He wished he could just forget about all those things and play with Meyote for a day or two. Even the smell of the cub somehow reminded him of little Miya, and he was filled with emotions of sadness and love and joy all at the same time. He knew that whatever happened, he would never forget these bears and these moments. He hoped the bears could remain a part of his life after the current crisis was over, if it ever got over.

There's so much happening around me that I don't understand, he thought. *Now, Mada is telling me that even she doesn't understand exactly what Rahwa is. I just wish I was home with my family. I hope going to see Rahwa's human friend is the right thing to do,*

"I'm glad to hear someone older and wiser tell me that. I've just been following him on instinct, and frankly, I'm not old enough to know how good my instinct is. I've felt I could trust him ever since we met, and so far it's been right. Do you know this human he's taking me to very well?" Dakar finally responded.

"Oh, yes. We've known Kattana for a long time. He's very wise. He's one of the last of the "true" Indians. He can still talk to us animals. He lives in the ways of the "old" Indians before the white-faced humans came to this land. I've been told that they appreciated and respected us much more than the humans do now. They could even talk to us like Kattana can, I hear.

109

Their lives were much like ours, living off the land and appreciating it. They didn't knock down the trees and build those horrid black trails with the hard surfaces. They didn't have those machines that belch noise and smoke. They were friendly and courteous. It's a shame things had to change. Kattana is a symbol of the way things used to be and what we can only hope we will see again someday. He'll know what to do to heal your shoulder. What we put on it will help it for a while, but it needs more than that gum."

Dakar felt reassured by Mada's words, and he said cheerfully, "I do feel much better for now. I think I'll go outside and see if I can find those ptarmigan you were talking about. I'll try to get enough for all of us, if I'm lucky."

As Dakar exited the den, it took several moments for his eyes to adjust the afternoon sunshine after being in the dark recesses of the bear den. He felt vulnerable since he wouldn't be able to clearly see any danger that might be lurking.

"Well, how's my traveling companion?" Rahwa shouted from a spruce tree nearby. "I hope that sleep didn't make your shoulder any stiffer."

As Dakar's eyes adjusted to the light he saw Rahwa in a tree, up about thirty feet with the light from the westerly sun shining on his black feathers. There seemed to be a glow radiating from Rahwa's body. The fresh smell of the green bushes being awakened by the spring thaw lifted Dakar's spirits. He felt recharged, and he now felt he was ready to handle the difficulties he knew would lie ahead. "Good afternoon to you, Rahwa. Have you by any chance seen any of those ptarmigan Sulman was talking about? I could do with a good meal right now, and I could try to get enough for the bears, too."

"Not ptarmigan, but I do know where some snowshoe hare are, and in addition, there are some pikas around there too. Those pikas look just like rabbits. I'd prefer you eat something besides a bird, if you can. Personal prejudice, you understand. That grouse you got earlier falls under the category of an emergency, you see. You needed the nourishment, and I didn't think you were going to be able to handle anything harder to catch. Anyway, just go up past that clump of bushes over to the right and you'll see a little clearing where the hares and pikas are eating some grass sticking through the snow."

Dakar was happy to be on a hunt. This was something familiar. While he had never *had* to hunt alone before, Torga had given him little projects occasionally to learn the skills he would need someday. He never knew he would need them this soon, and he was thankful for the foresight his father exhibited. He got as low to the ground as he could and crept past the bushes with only his nose and eyes exposed. There, on a small hill, he saw three hares and four pikas. He thought that if he moved carefully, he might get two of them at once. One would do him, and he could give the other as a present to his hosts. He made sure to have plenty of patience and to move very slowly. He had the advantage of having the sun at his back, so his profile was concealed by the strong light. He only moved one foot at a time, and it appeared he was just gliding along the snow with no apparent motion moving him. Soon, he was within striking distance, and he gathered his legs up beneath him, his hindquarters quivering in anticipation of the burst to come when he saw the majority of the hares putting their heads down to eat at the same time. This gave him as much advantage he could expect, and he burst forward in a blur of motion. The attack was swift and efficient. He had seized two of the hares before the others ran off, followed quickly by the pikas. He was proud of himself, and he had a twinge of sorrow that Torga and Tanya weren't there to congratulate him on a job well done. They were as good at praising him when it was deserved as they were at scolding when he misbehaved.

Dakar gathered the two hares in his mouth and started for the den. While his shoulder felt better than before Rahwa had put the gum on it, he could tell something was very wrong. He couldn't put any weight on it without a sharp pain shooting through his body. He knew then that he had no choice but to go with Rahwa to his Indian friend.

Rahwa was waiting with Sulman by the entrance to the den, and he smiled when he saw Dakar with his catch. "Not bad for a crippled cub, I'd say. You've got potential, kid," Rahwa said in praise.

"Sulman, I know it won't go far with your family, but I'd like to give this one to you," Dakar said as he dropped one of the hares in front of Sulman. "I hope someday I can do more to repay you for your kindness, but this is all I've got right now."

"Listen, little feller. We animals have to stick together, especially ones like you and me that the humans seem to want to eliminate. We lived in peace with them for generations, so I don't know why they think we don't belong on this earth any more. Goodness, I don't think I've even heard of a bear eating a human, and I haven't ever heard of you wolves ever eating one either. We occasionally get short tempered and run them off, but we don't eat them. I don't know why they consider us enemies. Live and let live, I say. I do appreciate the hare, though. I think I'll give it to Meyote. She hasn't had much meat; mostly berries and glacier lilies. It's time she tries some meat. It'll help her grow up big and strong."

Rahwa suddenly flapped his wings and turned his head first to one side, then the other, and finally said with alarm, "Listen, do you hear what I hear? I hear a drone that doesn't sound like an animal; it sounds like one of the human's machines!"

Sulman and Dakar stood very still and listened carefully. Finally Sulman said apprehensively, "Yes, I hear it. It's coming from the direction of the valley, and it's coming this way."

Dakar could just barely hear it, but it was increasing in volume, and finally Dakar said resignedly, "I know what it is! It's that terrible metal bird that the humans were in when they came down and tried to kill my family! Won't they ever leave us alone?"

Rahwa listened with his head cocked to the side for a second. "You know, I believe you're right. It does sound like one of those metal birds. They won't even leave the skies alone and let us use it in peace! They have to invade our space and take it for themselves too. I tell you what, now I'm getting mad! I think it's time for me to interfere with their plans. They've hounded you long enough, my little friend."

"Rahwa, what can you do? I appreciate your help and all, but you *are* a little bird! What we need is to get rid of that infernal metal bird," Dakar answered skeptically.

Rahwa looked at Dakar for a moment, and suddenly Dakar saw Rahwa's eyes start to glow. Dakar began to see what the eagle must have been seeing when he flew frantically away from the little raven. "What are you going to do, Rahwa?" Dakar said quietly as he looked away from the intense stare.

"Well, you've given me an idea. I think the skies are too friendly to those humans. I think I'll see if I can't do something about that," Rahwa answered, as he opened his wings and rapidly soared upward in the clear afternoon sky.

Dakar watched the raven zoom up, then fly in circles faster than Dakar had ever seen a bird fly. Rahwa rocketed out of sight to the west, then returned to view after five minutes. Suddenly, the sky darkened. Clouds appeared instantly, and the wind started blowing in Dakar's face. The snow shaking off the spruce trees kept hitting Dakar in the head. Finally, he had to stop looking up at the rapidly changing sky. The wind makes it difficult to hear the sound of the metal bird. Sulman showed his uneasiness, standing up on his hind legs and pawing at the sky.

"What is happening?" Dakar asked, his whole body trembling.

Sulman looked at Dakar, shaking his head in disbelief at the sudden change in the sky. "I don't know what is happening, but strange things always seem to happen when Rahwa is around. One thing I do know. Rahwa is behind all this. There are things about him we'll never understand. Just be thankful you met him. You'll find that out more and more as life goes on."

CHAPTER 12

Sanders held the plane in a steep climb as they went further into the MacDonald mountain range looking for an open flat spot where they could both land and takeoff. They were at 8,000 feet, and the plane didn't respond well at that altitude. The movements were slow and mushy in the thin air. Some of the mountain peaks were close to 10,000 feet, so Sanders had to keep the plane well clear of the peaks until he could find a suitable landing spot.

"It's a good thing the weather's so clear, mon ami. I can see the plane's not responding well at this level. I'm sure we'll see someplace soon we can put down," Tremaine said, sounding like he was trying to reassure himself.

"Jacque, look at that crazy bird next to us!" Sanders shouted. "I've never seen a raven up here at this altitude, and I didn't think they could fly this fast. He's just flying beside us, easy as you please, and durn if it doesn't look like he's staring at us!"

Just at that moment, the sky darkened, and they entered a cloud bank that had not been there seconds before. "Where in the world did this cloud *come* from? I was looking straight ahead just a few seconds ago, and it wasn't here! It must be just a little puff of cumulus. I'm sure we'll be out of it right away," Sanders told the group with forced confidence. "There's nothing forecast for anywhere near here today. I'm sure we'll be all right." His shaky voice gave away the fact that he wasn't as confident as he acted.

Tunnell's face looked like someone had drained the blood from his body. His skin turned ashen gray; his eyes were bulging and red. His lips were pursed in a tight grimace. His red hair seemed to reflect his fear as it flopped down over his eyes.

"Ben, are you okay?" Winslow asked with concern. "Don't worry, this is nothing but a little cloud. Didn't you hear what John said?"

"Yes, but nothing he has said so far has worked out right. Here we are in the middle of a cloud bank with a little single engine plane and a pilot that was cashiered out of the Mounties. Not to mention the fact that we are over a *huge* mountain range. Those aren't little hills down there like we have at home! Those are the real things, giant snow-covered mountains that will chew us up if we fall on them!" Tunnell muttered through tight lips.

"Now, boys, just relax. We'll be fine. We'll be out of this in no time," Sanders reassured them without conviction. "Maybe I'll just climb a bit more and see if we can't get on top of it. Then, we'll see just how big it is. We can always turn back and head for home."

Sanders pulled back the yoke of his steering column, and the plane responded reluctantly. They climbed to 10,500 feet, just about the limit they could fly for any extended period of time without oxygen. Sanders hadn't seen any necessity for bringing oxygen tanks on this trip, and the plane wasn't equipped with built-in oxygen.

Jacque looked out his window, and suddenly he let out a sharp gasp, saying, "I hate to bring any more bad news, but it seems ice is starting to build out here on this wing. How about yours, John?"

"Oh my God, you're right. We're not going to be able to hold this altitude with the weight we have on board and ice on the wings. Maybe I'd better turn back west and get out of this mess, if we can make it."

"WHAT DO YOU MEAN, IF WE CAN MAKE IT?" Tunnell shouted as loud as he could. "We just wanted to come out here, kill a couple of wolves, and go back to Oklahoma. We didn't ask to be up over some giant mountains with a couple of criminals in a tiny airplane and a pilot who doesn't know what to do about a few clouds! How did we ever get into this mess?"

Winslow shifted his weight uncomfortably. "Ben's got a point. What *are* we doing flying into some clouds over a mountain range with no oxygen and no deicing equipment? We *did* just come out here because you said you knew where we could get a couple of wolves, guaranteed."

"Look, you yellow cowards. You came to the Canadian Rockies. You wanted to go into an off-limits area and get yourselves some illegal wolves so you could go back home and tell your friends what heroes you are, and how you braved the great outdoors! Well, this is the great outdoors. I don't see you braving it very well. Maybe you should have just stayed home and killed a couple of stray dogs that looked like a wolf. Maybe that's all you can handle. Right now, I've got a problem I've got to handle, and your accusations and protests aren't getting us out of this cloud. SO, JUST SHUT UP!" Sanders responded forcefully.

Tunnell and Winslow glumly looked at each other, and neither knew what else to say. They looked out the windows, and nothing they saw gave them any comfort. The cloud appeared to be getting denser and darker.

Sanders turned around and looked at them carefully, saying, "I'm going to have to go down and find some place to put this thing. The ice is getting worse, and I can't hold this altitude. Unless one of you wants to jump out and lighten this plane, that's about my only option. Just keep quiet, let me do the best I can, and tighten your seatbelts. I don't want to scare you needlessly, but put your hands over the top of your head and pull your head down as close to your knees as you can." As Sanders finished his instructions, Tunnell heaved up the remainder of the contents of his stomach onto the floor of the plane.

Jacque looked at the scene in the back seat of the plane, and he said to Sanders, "Would you look at that gutless piece of jelly? If I get out of this alive, I'm going back to stealing or something else more respectable than this. Wet-nursing a couple of wimps is the worst occupation in the world. Anything, including prison, is better than this."

"Yeah, well, right now all I want to think about is getting us down in one piece. The controls are still mushy, and we're at 7,000 feet right now. I don't see any breaks in the clouds. Where did these clouds come from? One minute the sky was clear as a bell, and the next minute we're enclosed in a cloud bank. I've never seen anything like this before in my life. HOLD ON! I CAN'T HOLD MY ALTITUDE!"

The plane started a slow spiral down, down towards the unyielding mountains. Suddenly, they saw the steel gray and white specter of a mountain right beside them, and Winslow and Tunnell simultaneously let out a frightened gasp.

"We're going in!" Sanders shouted. "Hold tight!" Almost immediately, they felt a jolt and found themselves turned perpendicular to the ground, then flipped over on their heads. They heard crunching and sawing that they later knew to be large trees resisting the descent of the tiny plane. They were tumbled about the cabin despite their tightened seat belts. Then, they abruptly came to a halt upside down.

Sanders was the first one to get himself together enough to examine their predicament. He could tell he had a nasty cut over his eyes where the steering column hit him on impact. Also, his left arm felt numb. He looked around the cabin and saw that Tunnell and Winslow were either unconscious, dead, or so stunned that they couldn't move. Tremaine was clearly unconscious. Sanders saw that Tremaine's right leg was cut. Sanders found that all he could see outside the plane was snow, underbrush, and trees.

"How are you feeling?" asked Sanders, as he saw Tremaine start to regain consciousness. "Did you make it okay?"

"Mon Cher, none of us made it okay. You look like you just lost a fight with a bear, and I can't use my right leg. I don't even know if those clowns in back are alive or not. Don't much care, either. I don't think we're going to get any bonuses; probably won't even get paid. If not, they're just excess baggage."

Sanders rubbed some blood out of his eyes. "Well, the thought's appealing. I can tell my left arm has seen better days. Let's see if we can get one of the doors open. We do have enough gas in this plane to start a good fire. My door's crushed pretty badly, how about yours?"

Jacque tried his door. Sanders could see that the entire cockpit was bent somewhat, bending the door almost at the middle.

"Tell you what, Jacque. Let me get my legs over your waist, and I'll see if I can't kick the door open. You open the handle." As Jacque opened the handle, Sanders kicked at the door several times, and finally it popped open enough for them to crawl out. At Sanders' request, Jacque reluctantly reached back and loosened the seat belts on their passengers. Sanders had found that his left arm was essentially useless. Jacque tugged first one, then the other passenger out of the plane. They were still unconscious.

"They look like they're in better shape than we are," Sanders said after checking them over. "I bet they just hit their head on the top of the cockpit. There isn't much headspace in the back seat."

As he was talking, both passengers started moaning and slightly moving, assisted by the cold snow Sanders was rubbing on their heads and necks.

"Where are we?" Winslow asked. "I take it we're not in Heaven, if you two are still around."

"Well, Mr. Comedian, I hope you keep that sense of humor. We're God knows where, on some mountain in the MacDonald Range, and the only way we're going to get down is by foot. I already checked, and the radio is useless. Still got your sense of humor?" Sanders replied.

By this time, Tunnell had regained consciousness and was listening to Sanders' statement. "You mean you don't know where we are? Aren't there rangers or Mounties, or police or something around here?"

Tremaine looked at Tunnell with disgust. "Oui, Mister Great White Hunter. They're only about forty or fifty miles in some direction from here. Why don't you cry real loud and see if they hear you and come tuck you in while bringing your tea?"

"Okay, enough of that!" Sanders said adamantly. "We have to get down from here by ourselves, if we're going to get down at all. I only have one good arm, and Jacque only has one good leg. You two are in better shape physically than we are. We have to get lower before nightfall. None of us has any winter gear for a night up here on a mountain. We must get down as far as we can, then build some sort of igloo for the night. If you hold it together, and we work together, we should make it out of this alive. If you've never done it before, now is a good time to learn a little teamwork."

"Henry, if I we make it out of here, and I ever say anything about going to the mountains for any reason, please just get a gun and shoot my foot," Tunnell said.

"Once we get down? I'll be glad to do it now," Jacque injected.

Sanders listened to the exchange with disgust. "All right, fellows, settle down. We've got a tough walk ahead of us. We don't need to have this bickering."

"There's one thing no one has mentioned," Winslow interrupted. "There's the matter of the wolf. "I hope everyone here is with me on this, because I'm not leaving these parts until I've gotten him. He's not putting me through all this and getting away with it."

Sanders looked at Winslow with complete surprise. He hadn't thought Winslow had the determination he was showing. "If you're willing to keep after him once we get off of here, I'll stay with you. I'm starting to get mad, myself. One little 'ol wolf shouldn't be able to get away with putting us through this. I'd like to get his family, too."

Winslow looked at Tunnell. "Ben, how about you?"

"I guess you can count me in," Tunnell said resignedly.

"Well, the boys are growing up," Tremaine said with a sneer. "Going to stay with this hunt till it's finished, eh? Don't ever underestimate a wolf, though. They've survived a lot of people like us coming after them. They know we're here, so don't think this is going to be any easier than it has been up to now. However, if you don't give any more trouble and stay sober, I'll guide you till we get them. I'm getting tired of being made a fool by them, too."

The glare of sunlight made Sanders look up, and he exclaimed, "Would you look at that! Now, the sky's perfectly clear again! I've never seen weather change like that in my entire life!"

CHAPTER 13

Dakar looked at the sky, not sure he should believe his eyes. *How can a storm come up just like that?* Dakar thought. *If my father can't make something like that happen, and someone as strong as Sulman can't do it either, how could Rahwa possibly do anything like that?*

Dakar was getting very nervous, and he started for the opening to the den. He still had the hare in his mouth. He was carrying it into the den with him, as Sulman followed with the gift for Meyote. Just before Sulman entered the den, he looked back. He gruffed, "Look, Dakar. The storm's gone again."

Dakar turned and looked. He couldn't believe his eyes! The weather had just as suddenly cleared again, and the sun was out.

He stepped back out of the den opening just as a voice said, "Weren't worried, were you? Not afraid of a little bad weather, are you, my big, bad wolf?"

Dakar looked curiously at the tree just next to the den opening and saw the raven calmly preening his feathers; a look of total satisfaction and a smile across his face.

"That was *so* strange, the way the weather changed so suddenly. How could you possibly do that? Did you see where the metal bird is? Are they close? Do you think they know where we are?" Dakar asked nervously, the hair on his neck still elevated in fear.

"Calm *down*! Not so many questions! We won't have to worry about the metal bird and the humans inside it. They have other problems to deal with besides you for now. We can spend the night here safely, and then bright and early tomorrow we'll try to make it over the mountains to Kattana's home. You can rest easy for now," Rahwa answered casually.

"Who *are* you?" Dakar asked with a look of utter astonishment. "I'm so confused. There's just too much going on that I don't understand!"

Rahwa quit smiling, came down from the tree, and landed on a bush beside Dakar. He stretched out his wing and stroked Dakar's head. "There is a force in this world that helps those worthy souls that might make this a better place for those that come after. You've been chosen for that help, and I'm just the vehicle for that force. I'm supposed to help you learn things that will assist you in being a wise leader in the years to come. That's all you need to know, for now."

Dakar had felt a strange warm energy flow through his body as Rahwa stroked him. His shoulder didn't hurt nearly as much, and he had this feeling that his life really had meaning. He started to ask more questions, but Sulman touched his side with his huge paw. When Dakar looked up at him, he shook his head imperceptibly and said, "Let's give Meyote her food while it's still fresh. Just take Rahwa's word for it, you don't have to worry about *those* humans for now. If he says so, that's the way it is."

Dakar realized that Sulman felt no more questions should be asked. Dakar appreciated the bear's hospitality and friendship, and he didn't want to do anything that would offend his host.

They entered the den, and Dakar was happy to again be in surroundings that felt safe and familiar. Meyote was asleep with Mada resting beside her.

Mada smiled when she saw the strange group entering, and she saw the hare in Sulman's massive jaw. "What in the world are you going to do with that thing in your mouth?" she asked.

Meyote stirred when she heard her mother speak, and when she saw Dakar returning, she let out a little gruff-gruff-gruff, and then giggled as she bounced up and into Dakar, knocking him over.

"I'm about to show Meyote how to eat some meat. It's time she had some, and Dakar's gift is the perfect food for her first try." Sulman then gently pulled Meyote off Dakar, much to Dakar's relief. He turned her around so that he had her attention, then put the hare in her paws while keeping a small bit to show her what to do. She looked carefully at the strange object, then tentatively licked it. Soon, she was gulping it down with delight.

Dakar was happy he could do something to repay the hospitality of the gentle giants. His stay with them had been just the pause he needed during his journey. He would now be able to gather strength for the ordeal to come. In addition, the familiar family atmosphere of love and care made him sure that he would be able to get a good night's sleep. He knew he would need it for the journey over the mountains.

*   *   *

Torga lay in the snow for at least an hour. Whenever any of the pack looked like they were about to move, Torga gave them a stare; that was always enough. Finally, he gave a soft growl that meant it was all right to get up but not to leave the safety of the forest.

Tanya looked at him cautiously, then said, "You don't hear that metal bird anymore, do you?"

"No, but we can't be too careful when it comes to humans. Here in strange territory we don't know where to hide. I think it'll be all right to move now, but we'd better not go back to the moose. Remember, it was after a kill that those humans appeared last time," Torga answered. The pack whined when they heard Torga, for they had not yet finished their meal. Torga saw Pika and Tagar frown at each other, but they knew better than to say anything.

"We'll stay in the timber until we get back to Dakar's trail. Then, even if those humans are around, chances are they won't know where we are," Torga instructed. "Mutar, you better be the last in line. I know it's not your place, but I need you to watch our backside." Mutar, ever the loyal brother, coughed in compliance.

"Here's Dakar's trail," Torga announced. "He's marking it well. I guess he's hoping we'll come after him." Torga thought, *His schooling isn't near over, but he's doing very well. I'm so proud of him.*

"We've got to stay in the timber near Dakar's trail. We still don't know where those humans are," Torga continued. By this time of day, the melting snow slowed their progress considerably. Their feet would occasionally sink in the slush, even though their pads were covered with hair for just this reason.

Torga looked back at Tanya and said, "Are you sure you're up to this trip? It's a difficult journey. I could stay around here with you, and we could send the others ahead."

"Do I look like I can't keep up? I'm doing fine. I could probably out walk you. If you're getting tired, that's too bad. I'm going ahead. I can tell Dakar isn't feeling any too well, and I know you can tell it too. We've got to find him before something happens," Tanya said with a frown. Her lips were curled back, and her eyes were blazing with anger.

Torga could tell he had said the wrong thing. He stopped, turned around, and licked her mouth and let out little whines that softened her expression right away. He knew she couldn't resist this particular display of affection. He said, "I'm sorry. We'll keep going, but if you *do* feel tired along the way, be sure to let me know."

Torga found a path in the forest that was protected from the snow, and their pace quickened to about six miles per hour. This portion of the forest was alive with the mixed sounds of warblers, thrushes, Steller's jays, and boreal chickadees. Torga knew there were no humans about while the birds were so calmly announcing the beginning of spring with their songs. He could stay just parallel to Dakar's path, and they were making good time. He began to believe that they might catch up to Dakar before too long.

Suddenly, his hopes were dashed. He had gone over to Dakar's route to make sure he had stayed on course. He immediately smelled the scent-marking of another wolf pack. He knew it marked the beginning of the pack's territory. He gave a short whelp that made his pack hold perfectly still. He walked slowly over to them, saying, "I'm afraid we have a big problem. This is the boundary of another pack. We are not going to take a chance on running into them and having a fight. Not with Tanya about to have cubs. That means we'll have to go around their territory, and I don't want to take a chance on swimming across the river in open country. We'll have to go over the mountain to the east. I'm afraid this journey just got longer. We won't go any farther out of the way than we can help, but taking a chance on running into them on their territory is out."

Tanya was obviously upset. She spun around in small circles, and her tail twitched in every direction. Her eyes were large and unfocused. Finally, she calmed down enough to say, "Torga, does that mean that Dakar went into another pack's territory by himself? He wouldn't have a chance. If he weren't hurt, he might be able to outrun them; he's fast. But, what if he were hurt so badly he couldn't run away from them?"

"Calm down, Tanya. You know a pack doesn't necessarily kill an intruder just because he's in their territory. Remember that young wolf that came in our territory last fall. All I did was chase him until it was clear he was going to leave. That's what usually happens, particularly when it's a young cub like Dakar that isn't a threat to the leader. I'm sure Dakar will be all right. He knows enough to act submissive if he has to. Now, if it was Tagar, I'd worry," Torga said, as he smiled at Tagar, hoping a little humor might lighten Tanya's mood.

Tanya didn't even notice the reference to Tagar. She was obviously only thinking of Dakar, wounded and alone in strange territory. "Oh, Torga, let's do hurry. Set as quick a pace as you can. Don't worry about me keeping up. I won't rest easy until we've found our son."

CHAPTER 14

"Get up, Dakar! It's time to get started. It's daylight, and we have a long trip ahead of us. We should be able to make it to Kattana's home today if we hurry," Rahwa admonished.

Dakar slowly opened his eyes and looked at Rahwa with a complete lack of enthusiasm for Rahwa's urging. "Rahwa, it's still dark. I was sleeping so well, and you said I need to get lots of sleep." Meyote put a paw over Dakar's shoulder; she had slept right beside Dakar the entire night. It was obvious the little bear cub loved having Dakar for a playmate, and she must have sensed that Rahwa was trying to take her friend away.

"Dakar, you're in a den, dummy. You couldn't tell it was daylight in the afternoon. Trust me. It's daylight. You had a good night's sleep, and now it's time to move on. Get up!" Rahwa insisted.

Dakar stretched his body forward, then backward, loosening the stiff muscles. He was sore all over, for his sore shoulder had caused him to walk using other muscles. His left front leg was now almost useless. He smelled the now-familiar musky odor of the bears, and he knew he would miss their

137

companionship and friendship. He didn't know when he would again be with a family. He wondered if he could be happy staying with the bears, but he knew it wasn't his fate to live with bears. He wasn't sure why it wouldn't work out, but he knew he had a destiny to lead his family's pack. He had been taught to accept responsibility. He would never forget his new-found friends, and he hoped he would someday be able to come back to visit.

Sulman and Mada were awake, and they watched Meyote's expressions of affection for Dakar with pleasure. Sulman walked over to Dakar, and said, "I know you have to go. It has been great to have you in our family. You are welcome any time. When you are a grown pack leader, be sure to teach your pack that animals should be friends. Unless another animal is your food, there should be no reason to harm it. Rahwa has taught us that, and I'm sure he's teaching you the same thing. It's important!" Sulman gently put his gigantic paw on Dakar's back and bent over. Dakar gave him a mouth-licking. Sulman started to pull his head back, but instead he licked Dakar back with his huge tongue, licking Dakar's face from one ear to the other with one swipe. Dakar whined with pleasure.

"Dakar, we'll miss you," Mada said, "but not as much as our little Meyote will. It's too bad she hasn't learned to talk yet. She'd probably talk you into staying at least for a little while. We'd like that. She's going to be sad after you're gone; you're her first playmate." Mada then spontaneously reached down and effortlessly picked up the astonished wolf, holding him to her chest very carefully. She gave him one tremendous lick with her tongue, then set him gently down.

Dakar's eyes softened, and he let out a little howl, the first he had voiced since leaving his family. He had been careful not to do so before because of the danger from the hunters and the other wolf pack. Now he felt safe and sad. The bears' eyes likewise softened, and they each raised one paw in farewell. Dakar moved over to Meyote, who had a questioning expression on her face.

"I hope you can understand me, my dear friend. I'm going to come back to visit you some day, and even if you're a big grown bear you better remember me! I'll never forget you!" Spontaneously, Dakar licked her mouth again and emitted a soulful howl.

"All right, enough of this! If I introduce you to any more friends along the way, we'll never make it to Kattana's home.

Your shoulder will just fall off, or something," Rahwa said sarcastically. Rahwa put his face under his wing, so Dakar couldn't see how touched he was by the scene unfolding before him.

Dakar didn't reply. He just turned and slowly walked out of the den into the sunlight. He glanced back once and then started down the mountain. His shoulder was much worse than he had realized before he started walking. He now had to walk on three legs, and he could feel the heat returning to the wound. His whole body ached.

He walked slowly down the mountain through the spruce and pine thickets. He tried to stay away from the underbrush; it strained his shoulder when he had to blaze a trail through its unforgiving vines. Thankfully, the journey down was made easier by the frozen snow, which created a sort of sliding effect under his feet. They were on the western side of the mountain. The sun, rising in the east, had not yet gotten high enough to clear the peak of Mt. Haig, the mountain they were on. The snow would melt in the afternoon sun, then freeze over during the night. Dakar found that he could slide part of the way down the mountain by extending the pads on his feet so that the hair between his pads didn't slow his descent. Then, when he wanted to stop or slow down, he would simply tighten his feet so that his toenails and the hair on his feet would brake his movement. Once, before he became proficient with this procedure, he ran headlong into a chokeberry bush. Soon he learned he could only go short distances before he had to brake himself and start over. He reached the bottom of the mountain very quickly and waited for Rahwa to come down from the sky.

"That was a pretty good trick you used up there. I'm glad you saved your strength, because you've got a rough day ahead of you. What we're going to do is follow that trail right there by the river. The humans call it the Flathead River. You're going to stay on the trail until about midmorning. I'll be right above you. Then the tough part starts. We've got to go over that mountain range towards the sun. Kattana's home is just on the other side of the mountains. Not that it matters to you, but we'll be going from one of the humans' countries to another. Kattana lives in a place called Montana, on what the humans call a reservation. It's where the white-faced humans put all the Indians belonging to Kattana's family that they didn't kill. Believe me, Kattana and you have more in common than you have differences. You'll see. If you can keep going over the mountains without stopping too much, you might make it before nightfall. If not, we'll have to stay in the mountains. Some of Sulman's family live in those mountains, and we'll stay with them if it's necessary," Rahwa instructed Dakar in a very detached manner. *He must know I'm so lonesome since we left the bear family. He's keeping me focused on the journey to keep my mind off it,* Dakar thought. Dakar looked at Rahwa, stared deeply into his eyes, and said, "Don't worry. I know I need help. I'm going to make it over the mountains. I want to see my family and my pack again, and I'll do whatever it takes. Let me ask you a question: since you can do so many things, why can't you just make my shoulder better by yourself?" Dakar asked.

"I'm not allowed to change anything about any living being directly. I can only influence the elements around you and teach you things that can help you change yourself. It was decided long, long ago that all living beings are to have free choice on this world to be good or bad, smart or foolish, cowardly or brave. It's up to you. I can only make a difference if it's in you to be wise and strong anyway. If you can't make it to the Indians, I have no power to change that." Rahwa looked deeply and piercingly into Dakar's eyes, and Dakar knew that

Rahwa was doing everything he could to make the journey successful.

"Let's get going!" Dakar said with renewed energy. *I know now that I must finish this trip. If I can't do this, I'm not worthy of following my father*, Dakar thought. Dakar then started walking down the trail by the river, setting as fast a pace as he could maintain. He was going downhill, and he was energized by the knowledge that his destination was only a day away.

The journey was made more pleasant by the profusion of ducks of various types returning north from their migration. They were flying along the river's path, squawking in formation as they headed for the lakes they had left in the fall. He heard the honking of a flight of Canadian geese. Also in the sky were a variety of eagles, as well as osprey, all celebrating the coming spring after a harsh winter. The activity in the sky seemed to signify the reawakening of the countryside from a winter's sleep. Dakar could hear the grouse and white-tailed ptarmigan in the trees alongside the trail. There were beaver dams in inlets along the river, and he occasionally saw the industrious rodents working on their dams for the coming summer. He knew there would be game available if his hunger got unbearable. Right now his desire was to travel as far and as fast as he could. He had a goal to fulfill, and he wanted to do it as soon as he could.

They soon reached a spot where there was a visible trail going up the mountain. Rahwa flew down and landed in front of Dakar. "Whew, you really set a pace for yourself today. I know this is a hard trip for you. I hope you learn on this journey that in order to get anything worthwhile, you should expect to work hard for it. See that trail going up; that's where we're going. It's a trail the humans use in summer, but there won't be any of them around for at least another month. At the rate you're going, we should make it before night. You've got some rough climbing ahead of you, though," Rahwa said.

"Let's go! I want to get well, and then I want to find my family. Being with those bears reminded me that my family is the most important part of my life. I don't know anything but them, and my parents say it's the way of the wolf to always feel that way. I don't know if you can understand my feelings," Dakar answered with determination.

"Oh, Dakar, I understand very well. That's part of why I'm here. I want to make sure you find your family, never fear. You also need to learn that cooperation with others, including some humans, will benefit you and your pack. Let's start up the mountain. I imagine Kattana knows we're coming. He has the ability to sense things that are important. You'll learn to do that someday, too."

CHAPTER 15

Torga led his pack up the mountain and along a creek that he had found was the boundary of the wolf pack. He had Mutar walk right behind him, so that they would show their strength if they ran into the other pack. While the journey up the mountain was difficult, they felt more comfortable being away from any signs of human habitat. The thin air was fresh and free from smells of civilization. The cool wind energized the group, and the snow falling lightly on their backs from the spruce trees above also served to cool their backs.

Torga soon realized that the territory of the local pack was extensive; they would have to climb almost to the top of the mountain. The pack must be a big one, and therefore extra care would have to be taken to avoid an encounter.

At this altitude, the vegetation was sparse. There were isolated clumps of saxifrage and heather, but mostly barren rock and ice. There were occasional stands of Engelmann spruce. They saw several groups of rabbit-like pikas which lived amid the boulder fields at this altitude. The birds that were singing at the lower altitude were absent at this altitude, with only an occasional white-tailed ptarmigan or some rosy finches. They did see a group of about twenty mountain goats, but the goats would have been extremely difficult to catch in this environment. Also, the wolves weren't hungry, and they never expended the energy on a hunt in the winter unless food was necessary for their welfare.

Tanya got Torga's attention and said, "I feel terribly visible here in the open. Do we have to stay this high for long? What if the humans come around?"

"I don't think the humans will be at this altitude. I don't know where they could come down in that metal bird. It looks like it has to have a flat place to stop, and there aren't any up here. We'll be able to start down the slope in a little while. I don't think the pack's territory will extend this high for very long. Relax. At least it will be an easy trip down the mountain. I know you're worried about how Dakar got through the pack's territory, but he's smart. He'll make it," Torga assured her.

Just as Torga was beginning to head down the mountain, he heard a sound that sounded like thunder rolling down the mountain from above. He looked up to the peak of Mt. Marconi, and he saw snow rolling down the mountain in a huge wave, with a cloud of snow above the wave about sixty feet. It was rolling rapidly down right towards their location. An avalanche!

"Look up above! We've got to take cover!" Torga shouted.

In the springtime, with fresh snow falling on snow that has been frozen below, the fresh snow does not bind well with the older layers. It doesn't take a great deal of pressure to break loose one layer from another, creating an avalanche. The sound of the rolling snow was tremendous!

The pack panicked, but Torga whined loudly, "Follow me! We have to run right across the mountain. Don't go down! You'll never outrun the snow. We've got to get away from its path!"

The pack gathered itself, and they ran with remarkable speed borne of dire necessity. Torga got to a clump of spruce that he was sure was outside the path of the slide, and when he looked back, his shoulder hairs rose and his ears stood erect, for he saw that little Pika had fallen behind and the snow had gathered her and was hurling her down the slope at a horrifying speed. Torga could see the look of panic in her eyes as she was rolled under, then spit to the top of the wave of white horror.

"Quick, we've got to follow the snow down! Pika's caught up in it!" Torga yelled to the pack. He stole a quick look at Tanya and was sorry that he had. She looked so scared! Her eyes were wide, and her tail was flickering in all directions; she was jumping up and down with nervous energy. Then, she tore down the mountain after the slide with no concern for pack discipline or for her own safety.

The avalanche stopped in a grove of timber about two hundred yards down the mountain. Pika was nowhere to be seen. Tanya, the first wolf at the scene, started sniffing quickly all over the thirty-foot pile of snow. Suddenly, she stopped and turned to the pack, which had just arrived, saying, "Here! I can smell her! She's right in here somewhere!"

Torga led the pack in digging at the spot Tanya had designated. He never thought to question her judgment; he had known her too long. If that was where she said Pika was, that's where she was. No time to check it out. They dug frantically, and soon Mutar whined, and they saw a leg sticking out where he was digging. They all rushed to that spot and had her free in seconds.

Tanya started licking her face, and Torga was pushing on her chest with his front feet. At first, she didn't move at all, and the pack paced around in desperation. Suddenly, Tanya saw her head move slightly. Tagar saw it at the same time, and he let out a whelp without thinking.

Torga's head swung towards the cub, and he snarled, "Tagar, we're in another pack's territory! Hush! They'll be coming to check on the noise from the snow slide anyway."

Tanya was busy licking her cub's face and pushing on her with her nose. Soon, Pika slowly opened her eyes, and said, "Mommy! Am I all right? I was *so scared*! That horrid snow just threw me around like I was a piece of bark! I just stopped to look at it for a minute, and it was on top of me! I don't want to *ever* feel like that again!"

Torga came over, licked her affectionately on the mouth, then said, "Pika, when there's danger about like that, you can't afford to stop and look at it, whatever it is. That's my responsibility. When I say to run, you have to just follow my lead. You learned a valuable lesson today, and thankfully it wasn't too hard a lesson. You're lucky, but you may not be so lucky again."

"Torga, I just heard the sounds of the local pack! They're coming up from that stand of pine to the right," Mutar said breathlessly, as he rushed up from his guard position down the mountain. Mutar, Torga's brother, had taken up position between the pack and any expected danger without being told. It was a procedure that was routine within the pack.

"All right, they are probably coming because of the noise of the avalanche. They probably don't know we're here. Quickly, let's go! Follow me down the mountain to the south. We can outrun them until we get outside their territory. I don't want to fight with them if we can help it!" Torga growled quietly. "Are you able to run, Pika?"

"Yes, I'll be all right. I'm just shaken up. Don't worry, I won't lag behind again. I've learned my lesson," Pika answered. Torga had already taken off as soon as Pika said yes.

The local pack arrived at the site of the avalanche not long after Torga and his pack had left. They looked the snow hill over, trying to decide what had created it. By the time one of their members had noticed the scent of Torga and his family, they were well down the hill.

Torga bounded through the snow without any concern for what danger might be in front of him. There were times when any possible danger had to be overlooked, when they were fleeing from a known peril. The melting snow enabled the wolves to run full speed, for each step was partially braked by the soft yielding mush. They tore through a group of chokeberry bushes and then fell headlong into a small depression. They never broke stride, rolling back into an erect position and continuing down, ever down away from the pursuing pack. They could hear the pack yelping, for there was no need for the pursuers to maintain stealth. They knew Torga's pack was running from them. While Torga's pride made him want to stand and fight, his good judgment told him there was nothing to fight over. He didn't want to take their territory. He saw no reason to try to tell them that unless he was forced to; better to just get away. Finally, as they came to a river, Torga smelled the scent-markings telling him that the river was the edge of the pack's territory. They ran along the edge of the river, which was flowing the same direction they were running, until the scent-marks showed him the southern boundary of the pack.

Torga stopped and watched as his pack came running up. They were all there, and Pika was right behind her mother. "All right, we're out of their territory. Now, I know we're east of Dakar's route. I know Dakar didn't try to go around the wolf pack's territory; we would have picked up his scent. He must have made a run right through, staying on his course by the river. We'll just head back to the west until we find his trail. Each of you keep searching as we go. We need to find his trail before dark, while it's still very fresh. I can smell human dens in front of us, so be very careful."

They had stopped about five miles from a town of humans.

*   *   *

Sanders was laboring under the weight of Tremaine's body. Tremaine had his right arm around Sanders on the journey down the mountain, for he couldn't use his right leg. Sanders now wished he had taken the time to try to find his large knife somewhere in the back of the plane; maybe he could have cut a walking stick for Tremaine. They didn't even have their guns, which they hadn't been able to find in the debris of the crash. It was really bad luck that the tail of the plane, where they stored all their gear, had received so much damage.

"How much farther do we have to go?" asked Tunnell, who was puffing heavily under the weight of his own body. "I don't know how much further I can go."

"Well, there's a solution to that," Jacque answered. "Why don't you just sit down and stay here until summer?"

"All right, you guys." Winslow interjected. "It's going to be tough enough to make it down without bickering. Let's make the best of a bad deal and just get off this mountain as fast as we can. Ben, it's plain these would-be guides don't know what they're doing, so don't bother to ask them any questions." Sanders said nothing, for what he wanted to say wouldn't help matters any. It was a hazard of his type of business that he was stuck with the scum of the earth. *I guess I have to admit,* he thought, *that I'd be upset too if I hired a pilot that crashed the plane. I still don't know where all those clouds came from or where they went so suddenly.*

They were making their way down a ridge that seemed to have less snow on it, due to the fact it was exposed to sunlight all afternoon. The footing was better, and they were making decent time. They had traveled about half-way down the mountain, when they went through a spruce grove. Winslow had been walking in front since the last exchange between the groups, showing his irritation by taking the lead. All of a sudden Sanders saw Winslow stop still, and Sanders could see his whole body shake. Winslow turned around slowly, and his face was as white as the snow beneath him. His eyes were wide, and his expression of horror made Sanders wonder if he were having hallucinations.

"There's a HUGE bear right around the bend of the ridge!! I didn't know bears could GET so big! Quick, John, come take a look. What do we do?" Winslow looked like he was about to fall faint in the snow. His knees were shaking so much his khaki pants were making sounds like a sail in the breeze.

"Just hold perfectly still, Henry. Let us come down slowly and take a look. Don't run, whatever you do!" Sanders and Tremaine slowly made their way down the ridge and through the last few trees to Winslow's location.

What they saw gave them no comfort. There, not thirty feet from them, was not one bear but two grown bears and a cub. The larger bear, obviously the male, was chomping his jaws and making a "woofing" sound while putting his head down with his ears laid back.

"See those movements the big bear is making?" Tremaine said, "Well, that's not good. That shows he is being aggressive and is thinking about attacking us."

"OH NO!" Tunnell exclaimed. "Tell me this is a nightmare! If I ever make it off this mountain, I swear I'll never get on another one!"

"Thank God." Tremaine replied. "We're the last unlucky souls that will have to put up with you. For now, though, I suggest we slowly back away. Don't turn your back to them, whatever you do. And DON'T run. You don't have a chance of outrunning him. If you can climb, look for a tree to climb. Adult grizzlies can't climb trees. If the cub climbs after you, though, the parents will wait at the bottom for you no matter how long it takes. Neither John nor I have a chance of climbing, so we're going to slowly back away and head down the mountain."

"I gather there are no good choices, right?" Winslow answered resignedly. "If that bear gets me, it's not going to be pulling my butt off a tree. I think I'll take my chances with you two, okay Ben?" Tunnell could only nod; he looked like he was going into a trance, his eyes wide and unfocused.

As they slowly backed away, the mother bear put her nose in the air and swung her head from side to side. She was making "woofing" noises that the hunters, of course, couldn't understand.

"Sulman, these must be the humans Rahwa and Dakar were talking about. I know you are thinking about hurting them, but that will just cause us trouble. We've got to think about Meyote."

"Don't forget, Mada, they tried to kill Dakar's family. Don't you think they deserve to be hurt?" Sulman answered with a woof.

"Of course they do, but I don't want you to do it. Maybe just scare them a little bit. That ought to keep them from coming around us for a while."

"Listen, that male looks like he's going to charge. The only chance you have is to play dead by clasping your hands on the back of your neck, lying down, and curling up. Remain quiet! Keep that position until he leaves!" Tremaine said quietly.

"Oh my God!" Winslow managed to mutter.

Sulman then charged at the hunters with unbelievable speed for a nine hundred pound animal. He covered the forty feet between them in a flash, and the humans all fell down in a clump of tangled legs, arms, and snow. Sulman then growled and walked slowly back to his family.

"THAT'S IT!" Tunnell muttered. "I'm going down this mountain, finding a way back to Oklahoma, and I never want to see any of you people again! Including you, Henry!" Tunnell then got up, dusted the snow off his body, and started walking down the ridge with the look of a man with a goal.

157

"Wait a minute, Ben," Winslow called. "We've still got the matter of a wolf and his family. We aren't going to let them get the best of us, are we? What would our friends in Oklahoma say if I told them you ratted out on the hunt?"

Tunnell turned and looked at Winslow with an angry stare. "You wouldn't do that, would you?"

"We're in this until we get those wolves. That's what we pledged when the plane went down, and I'm holding you to it."

"Well," Tunnell hesitated, "I *would* like to get even with those wolves. Just till we get them, okay?"

"Right."

CHAPTER 16

Dakar began climbing the barely visible trail. He could smell the tracks of many humans and animals that had used the trail before, even through the snow. He found that it was easier to follow the smells than it was to pick out the trail by sight.

They had about thirty-five miles to travel before they reached the other side and the Blackfoot Indian Reservation. Within an hour they had reached Kintla Lake, which was still partially frozen over. There were a multitude of varieties of birds; white pelicans, whooping cranes, great blue herons, cormorants, gulls, and most species of North American ducks. They had begun arriving from their winter migration.

Dakar called to Rahwa, who was flying overhead. When he descended, Dakar asked, "Why is this part of the countryside so attractive and preserved from the signs of humans? All the way here, we could see signs of humans destroying the land, but here it looks like nothing has been changed."

Rahwa smiled. "This is one of your lessons, my friend. *Humans* made sure this land would stay in its natural state for everyone to enjoy. Some humans *do* care what happens to the land, and this is one of the results of their concern. They even made sure the animals here are protected. This is what they call a National Park, and they call it Glacier. As we get further up the mountain, you will see glaciers around. Glaciers are areas where the snow and ice never melt. There *is* hope for humans to one-day return to the *real* values of all animals, including them. This is one of the signs of it."

"Well, I guess I've got a lot to learn. But I'm just a young wolf. I'd love to forget about all these serious things for a while and just stay here and look at all those birds."

"Look, Dakar, if you wanted to become a tourist, you didn't need me," Rahwa complained from his perch on a tree above. "We're barely going to make it before dark without you stopping to gawk at all the birds. Goodness, you've got me to look at. Isn't that enough?"

"Sorry, Rahwa. I didn't know I was hurting your feelings. I haven't seen many of those birds before, and I've never seen so many birds in one place in my life!"

"As much as you hate to admit it, you aren't in very good shape. Look at you. You're now walking on only three legs. You need help. While you're recuperating, you can come back here and look all you want. There are lots of lakes between here and Kattana's home, and they all have plenty of birds. This area is pretty safe for you this time of year. You don't have to waste *my* time with your sightseeing."

Dakar could tell he had upset Rahwa. He didn't know what to do. His normal response would be mouth-licking in apology, but that was obviously out of the question. "Rahwa, are you hungry? I saw some of those animals you call a pika over by those rocks. I could probably catch one, if you want it."

"No, Dakar. I ate some berries at the bear's den. I'm fine. Let's just keep going."

He realized that Rahwa was right, that he needed to get to the medicine man's home as quickly as possible. His shoulder was hurting worse, and he felt hot even though there was snow all around. He didn't stop to enjoy the scenery any more. It was difficult, for the landscape was magnificent. There were serrated ridges and horn-shaped peaks overlooking turquoise lakes; there were waterfalls, cascades, meadows, and wildlife everywhere. He saw bighorn sheep and mountain goats up above the trail at several spots. He saw several varieties of deer, and he smelled the scent of several coyotes. It occurred to him that Torga and Tanya would love it here, and he hoped he could bring them here someday. He went over Boulder Pass and then passed Waterton Lake. He stopped to admire the lake's beauty, but a disapproving look from Rahwa told him he had to be on his way. He was more tired than he had ever been in his life, and his shoulder was getting worse with every step. He understood why Rahwa was so anxious to get to the medicine man today.

Rahwa must know how bad my shoulder is, Dakar thought. *If I slept here overnight, I might not be able to walk at all tomorrow. I hope Kattana can tell me how Rahwa knows so much.*

Finally, just before dark, Rahwa came down to the trail in front of him, and said, "You really did well to walk this far today. I know you're going to make a great leader, and I know your family will be very proud of you, Dakar. See that mountain just to our north; that is called Chief Mountain by the humans. It marks the edge of the Blackfoot Indian Tribe's home. We're almost at Kattana's house. You will really like Kattana. I promise you. Also, he has a daughter named Anatoki. She is young, like you. She is about fourteen years old, which is about the same age as you are in wolf years. All we have to do is follow this trail for about half an hour more. We will have completed our journey!"

"You mean there are two humans I'll have to deal with? What else haven't you told me? Rahwa, this has been a long, hard trip. I hope I was right to trust you."

"Don't worry, Dakar. Everything will be all right now. I promise you. This trip will be the most important thing that will ever happen in your life. Remember I said that."

* * *

Torga picked up Dakar's trail not too far from the highway Dakar had crossed. Tanya came over to him when he whelped out the sign he had found the scent. She started licking his mouth in the excitement of knowing that Dakar had made it through the wolf pack's territory. She turned her body sideways to his and rubbed up against him with her tail held high.

"Tanya, calm down! We've got a long way to go before we're united with Dakar. He made it through one hurdle, but there's plenty to worry about before we find him. We still don't know where those humans are with the metal bird. It's almost night, and I don't want to travel in strange country after dark. We've got to find a safe place to stay for the night. Now that we know Dakar's all right up to here, we can worry about our own safety. Let's head over toward the mountains and find someplace to make a temporary den. Then we'll get started in the morning."

The happiness Tanya felt could be seen in the smile on her lips and the twinkle that had returned to her eyes. "Now that I know Dakar was strong enough to make it here, I'm *sure* he'll make it to wherever he's going. I wonder where he *is* going? He should have lost those humans by now. He seems to have someplace special he's heading for, but he doesn't *know* anything except our territory."

Torga felt much better now that he could see the confidence returning to Tanya. He patiently listened to her, then said, "Well, it's hard to understand what a cub on his own will do. Don't forget, he's less than a year old. He might have gotten disoriented and think he's heading for home. We'll know when we find him. Right now, let's worry about you and the little cubs inside you."

Torga sent Mutar up ahead to scout a likely location while he stayed back with the pack to protect Tanya and the cubs. Soon, Mutar came back with word that he had found a satisfactory den in a spruce grove up the slope. They preferred being in spruce forests, for it was familiar to them; their den at home was in a spruce forest. Mutar showed the way, and they denned up for the night.

I know we've only got a day or two before we have to make a den for Tanya, Torga thought. *I hope we catch up to Dakar tomorrow. It's soon going to be too late to continue the search.*

CHAPTER 17

Dakar was now unusually agitated, for he was about to meet a human for the first time. His tail twitched involuntarily, and his eyes darted from side to side. Rahwa led him down the trail past Chief Mountain about three miles to a road—a path really—that ambled along a creek. They passed a grove of various trees: cedar, hemlock, and pine. Just past the trees and hidden from view from the road or trail they came upon a dwelling. It had a warm, comfortable feeling with its vine-covered chimney, its unusual stone walls, and a porch around the outside with a swing attached to the ceiling. Smoke curled invitingly from the chimney. There were many signs of human habitation about: a bicycle on the porch, an old automobile parked next to the house, and a barn just beyond the house. Dakar saw a corral next to the barn and horses in the corral.

"What are those animals?" Dakar asked. His eyes were wide with wonder, and his body was shaking with apprehension. "I've never seen anything like that before."

"Those are horses. They are harmless to someone like you. Humans use them for transportation. They get on their backs and ride them. Quit worrying!" Rahwa admonished.

A dog came out from behind the house and walked towards Dakar and Rahwa.

Dakar immediately stood tall with his ears and tail erect and his mouth open with the corners pulled forward. He bared his teeth and emitted a low growl. "Take one more step and I'll chew you into little pieces, stranger."

"Calm down, Dakar," Rahwa said quickly. "I forgot to tell you about him. He's called a Rottweiler, and years of breeding made him look different from you, but he's related. His name is Auatuyi; it means wags-his-tail in the Blackfoot language. That doesn't sound like a dangerous animal, does it?"

"Are there others in his pack?" Dakar asked uneasily.

"He's a dog; wolves are their ancestors, but they have been domestic possessions of humans for thousands of years. They haven't traveled in packs since they were domesticated. They aren't much like you any more, but I'm sure you can understand each other. Inside, they still have a lot of the same instincts you have."

Auatuyi smiled at Dakar. "Easy there, little wolf. I don't want to hurt you. We've been expecting you. Kattana said this morning we would have unusual guests for dinner. He's inside preparing food for you."

"How did you know I was coming? I don't understand what is going on, and I don't like someone I don't know calling me 'little wolf'," Dakar said menacingly.

"Relax. This is a peaceful place, and you shouldn't come in here with all that hostility. I understand your body language, and I could whip your butt if I wanted to, but I want to be friends with everyone, just like my master. I've been taught that violence doesn't get you anywhere."

"I'm sorry," Dakar said. "I have been taught that everything and everyone but my family is either a danger or food. I'm just beginning to meet animal friends like Rahwa here and my new bear friends. This is all new to me. Tell me, what is a master?"

"Well, I've been told about you wolves. You don't have anything like a master, unless you'd call your pack leader one. My master is Kattana, and he provides everything for me. I pretty much do whatever he tells me to do, but he doesn't tell me to do very much. We're more like friends, but he's in charge. I guess your pack leader is pretty much like that. Then

168

there's Anatoki, his daughter. I guess we're more like playmates. You'll love her. Her name means pretty head, and she *is* beautiful. She's also kind and sweet and gentle. Just don't do anything to hurt her, or you'll really see how angry I can be!"

"Don't worry," Dakar quickly responded. "If something isn't an enemy or food, we wolves don't ever hurt it. My father tells me he's never heard of a wolf killing a human; he doesn't understand why they always want to kill us. That's why I'm so leery of meeting a human; this will be the first one I've ever met. I've been taught that they are bloodthirsty animals that will kill anyone and everything!"

"You'll find someone quite different from that when you meet Kattana and Anatoki," Auatuyi responded with pride. "They're two of the gentlest, kindest creatures there could be!"

"Here, now. I think my guests have arrived!" a human's voice shouted from the porch. He had stepped outside so silently Dakar hadn't even noticed. "You must be the wolf my dreams said would be arriving. And hello to you, Rahwa. The moon has set many times since I last saw you. I've missed you. Anatoki will be glad you two have finally gotten here. I told her several days ago about my dream. I dreamed last night you would be here today, but we were about to give up. She sometimes doesn't have as much faith in my dreams as she should." Kattana shook his head sadly.

Dakar had jumped back when he heard Kattana's voice. He had never heard a human speaking to him. Kattana had just kept talking, although he obviously saw Dakar's movement. There was something about him that was very reassuring, just like when he met Rahwa. "I didn't think we could understand or talk to humans. My father told me they didn't understand us, and we didn't understand them. Why can I understand you?" Dakar asked tentatively.

"Your father was right for the most part, little wolf. At one time, animals and men were able to understand each other. Then man decided to leave the ways of nature and honor for the ways of greed and selfishness. Now we try to talk to you, but you don't reply, except in dreams. There are a few of us Indians who still practice the old ways, and we never embraced civilization as the white-faces practice it. We still have the ability to communicate with our animal friends, for we aren't corrupted with the new way of life. Unfortunately, there are fewer and fewer of us. Here, there are only about sixty of us left who practice the old ways. We were once about 40,000."

Dakar finally collected himself and took a good look at Kattana. He was middle-aged, and he carried himself with dignity, like an older pack leader who had retired with honor. His hair was long, down to his shoulders and flecked with gray streaks. His shoulders were broad, and his eyes were sharp with a gentle edge. His skin was wrinkled, but the wrinkles around his eyes were shaped in a permanent smile that made his gentleness more obvious. While he wore the clothes of the humans Dakar had seen before, he wore a necklace of quills and beads that seemed to fit his true personality better. It was like the clothes were a costume, and the person within wasn't really meant to wear them. Dakar was surprised that he felt so comfortable with Kattana; he had been prepared to be very defensive.

Just at that moment the front door opened and out walked a young girl. "Hi, there! I'm Anatoki!" she shouted. "I see father was right. You *did* come today." Dakar hadn't known what to expect, of course, but he wasn't prepared for what he felt when he saw her. She immediately gave him the same indescribable feeling of trust that he had felt when he first met Rahwa. She had long black hair that she wore straight, and it went down almost to her tiny waist. She had on a white T-shirt that served to highlight her smooth olive skin. The T-shirt was tucked into form-fitting blue jeans. Her face radiated a sense of peace and tranquility. Her smile washed her whole face, and it was the most open, natural smile Dakar could have imagined.

I've never seen a more beautiful smile on any creature, even a wolf, Dakar thought. *Why do I want to lick her mouth in greeting, when I don't even know her?*

"Oh, this is the wolf of your dreams, papa? What a beautiful wolf he is!" Anatoki exclaimed. "Come say hello, E-muck-o-tis-ah-pi-ce-yi!"

Dakar was surprised that he knew she was calling him "little wolf" in the Blackfoot language. He could tell that this was to be a visit with many surprises in store. Without thinking, Dakar strode over to her and said, "You, you are so beautiful! I had no idea a human could be so lovely!" As he spoke, he rubbed against her leg, and when she knelt down, he instinctively gave her a lick that went from her chin to her forehead.

Anatoki was startled for a second. Then, she let out a delighted giggle that made Dakar feel like he was floating on a cloud. "You are such a sweet little wolf. Come, Papa, we must bring him inside and tend to this awful looking wound on his shoulder!"

Dakar felt at that moment that he would have followed her anywhere she asked him to go. He felt an emotion he hadn't known existed. It was almost like the love he had for his parents, but not quite. It was almost like the protective love he had felt for his dear sister, Miya, but much more intense. He was terribly confused. Suddenly, the release of the tension he had felt together with the strain of the trip made him very weak, and he collapsed in Anatoki's arms. He whined, "Oh, I'm sorry. Forgive me. I guess my shoulder is hurt worse than I've been willing to admit."

"Papa!" Anatoki cried. "Our little wolf is hurt badly! We must do something quickly! Help me carry him!" At that moment, Anatoki saw Rahwa standing on the walk, looking very unhappy.

"Oh, Rahwa, I'm sorry. I didn't mean to ignore you," Anatoki said as she noticed Rahwa's disappointment. "I was just so surprised to see such a magnificent creature. I didn't know there was anything so handsome in the world. And, he needs our help so badly!"

Dakar felt as comfortable in Anatoki's arms as he felt when he was lying next to his mother in their den, but there was a feeling now that he didn't have when he was with his mother.

"Everything all right, Dakar?" Rahwa asked with a sly grin. "You seem nervous, *or something.* I *do* hope it wasn't a mistake to bring you here."

Dakar looked at Rahwa, and he knew that Rahwa could tell what he was feeling. "You were right, Rahwa. I admit it. Coming here may be the most important thing to happen in my life. These people don't seem to be at all like any of the humans I have heard about before. I'm beginning to learn that you can't put humans into a group and believe they're all terrible creatures."

"Oh, is Dakar your name?" Anatoki asked. "What a pretty name. Your parents must love you very much, and I can see why. I don't blame you for being leery of humans. You should be. You'll find that the attitude of our tribe is quite different towards animals than that of many other humans. We have always loved and respected animals. Papa tells me that in early days, before the white-faces came, we kept cranes, hawks, eagles, beavers, antelope, and yes, even wolves in our tipis. He said some Indians have even kept grizzly bears in their tipis.

Would you let me keep you in my tipi, Dakar?" Anatoki asked with an innocent grin.

"Uh, uh, uh, sure, I would. And nothing would ever be able to harm you while I was there, either!" Dakar said with his chest puffed out.

"You're really the big, bad wolf now, aren't you, Dakar?" Rahwa asked impishly.

Dakar could feel the blood rush to his head. *I can't believe how protective I feel towards a human I thought I wouldn't even like only a few minutes ago,* he thought. *Why am I like water in Anatoki's hands?*

"Don't you tease him, Rahwa. The poor dear has a terrible wound. Papa, we must get him inside the house. You *can* take care of his wound and make him feel better, can't you, Papa?" Anatoki asked.

Kattana's eyes twinkled, and he said, "I have some medicines for his wound, and I get the feeling that with you looking after him, he'll feel better in no time. Come, let's carry him inside and get to work on that shoulder."

Dakar let the two humans he had thought he could never like carry him inside. Anatoki's touch made the pain of his shoulder much more bearable, and he found himself trusting

Kattana completely. He knew his shoulder would get good treatment now.

Auatuyi, who had been silent during the introductions and exchanges between his masters and the visitors, now came up beside Dakar as they were carrying him. "Well, I told you how great my mistress is. I don't have to ask you whether you agree or not. I think I'll be able to take some time off from my guard duties while you're around. I have the feeling no one will get close to Anatoki except the family now," Auatuyi added.

"I'm sorry I acted so unfriendly when we met. I wasn't expecting to meet humans like Kattana and Anatoki. Nothing I've known or been told prepared me for your pack. I promise I'll help you take care of Anatoki," Dakar replied sincerely.

Auatuyi looked at Dakar with a smile and said, "I have no doubt about that, Dakar. I think we will be friends. When you feel better, I'll teach you how to play with balls and toys."

"Okay, you guys," Anatoki said. "You'll have plenty of time to talk about playing after we've taken care of Dakar's injury and he's rested up. He's going to need lots of rest. Do you mind sleeping in the house, Dakar? If you stay in my room, I can take care of you during the night."

"NO! I don't mind. A house is just kinda like a den, isn't it? We live in a den all the time. I'm more used to being inside than I am sleeping out in the open."

"Well, it sounds like we're not going to have any trouble getting to know one another," Kattana said with a smile. "Let's get you into the kitchen, Dakar. I've got some things that I believe will fix your shoulder. Don't worry, Anatoki is coming too. You too, Rahwa."

Rahwa hesitated. "I'll come in for a little while, but I don't want to sleep in the house. I've never gotten used to being where I can't fly if I want. I'll stay while you fix him up, but I don't believe Dakar is going to need me around for support very long. Are you Dakar?"

Dakar looked at Rahwa carefully. He wanted to make sure that Rahwa didn't think he was being ignored during all the excitement of meeting humans and finding he liked them. "Rahwa, you've been a very good friend, the best that a wolf could ask for. I don't know what would have happened to me if I hadn't met you, but I know it wouldn't have been nearly as pleasant or safe. I'll always want you around, if you'll stay."

"Well, Dakar, our meeting wasn't an accident. It was destiny. I've done about all I need to do for you now. I think you're learning the things I wanted you to learn. I'll stick around until tomorrow. Then, we'll see."

Dakar's face dropped. *I don't feel so happy any more,* Dakar thought. *It hadn't occurred to me that Rahwa would leave me.* Even though they had only met a few days ago, their adventures together had created a bond that only shared adventure and danger can create.

Kattana looked at Dakar's wound. "Well, Dakar, I can see that this wound is caused by a gunshot, and part of the bullet is still in you. That's what's causing your pain; it's called infection. First, I'm going to wash it out, then I've got to take the metal out. It's going to hurt, so don't get mad and bite me."

Dakar turned his head with a start. *I'm not sure if I should let any human, even Kattana, dig into my shoulder,* he thought.

Rahwa looked at Dakar with a stern stare. "Do as he says, Dakar!"

"Okay," Dakar said timidly. *I've trusted Rahwa this far, and it's worked out. I guess I'll trust him some more.*

Kattana quickly went to work. He washed the wound, then took a thin, very sharp knife with a bone handle that looked very old and very used. He dug into the wound, put his index finger in beside the knife, and came out with a round piece of metal.

"Yelp!" Dakar whined, as Kattana dug into him. However, he used all his discipline and kept himself from instinctively snapping at Kattana.

"Well, the worst is over," Kattana said with a satisfied look. "Now, the first thing I'm going to put on that wound is some Ana-wawa-toks-tima, or yellow cancer root. I can see that Rahwa found some fir gum to use during your trip. That helped, because the infection isn't as bad as I was afraid it might be. Hold still, now." Kattana chewed the root until it was a mash, and then he blew it upon the wound. "Next, I'll use some oks-pi-poku, or sticky root. I have some here already ground up." He put a little water in a dish, put some of the ground root in the dish, then put the mixture on the wound. "The last thing I'll use tonight is some apos-ipoco, or alum root. It'll take some of the swelling and soreness out. Anatoki will put some of this on during the night, too." He then applied this ground root just like he had the previous mixture.

"All right, little friend. The last medicine I'm going to give you is something for your insides. This treat is something I'll bet you've never tried, but you'll like it. It's called a chicken, and it tastes somewhat like a grouse. I know you've had grouse, coming from that area in the Kootenay Mountains. Yes, I know where your home is. I know you must be hungry. Anatoki, get some chicken out of the fridge, please. And get some for Rahwa, too."

Rahwa looked at Dakar with a wide smile and said, "How do you like my choice of healers so far, my friend?"

"Now, I know why we had to make such a difficult journey. You were right, Rahwa. You've been right this whole trip, but I still don't know why you bothered with me. You told me I'd know later, but I don't."

"Yes, you do. You just don't realize it. See how much you like two humans you thought you would hate? Well, humans used to feel the same way about wolves. They're beginning to learn about wolves what you learned about humans on this trip. The more you two animals get to know one another, the more you'll find how much you have in common. There are good and bad humans and good and bad wolves. You're going to be a leader, and you'll be a better leader now that you know you can count on some humans. There are others teaching the same thing to human leaders. For right now, just eat and get well."

Now, I see what Rahwa was doing, bringing me here, Dakar thought. *I wonder if he could have healed my shoulder himself?* Dakar didn't realize how hungry he was. He was safe and comfortable with no worries about what lay just ahead for the first time since he began his journey. He ate very well. He didn't know if it was the chicken that was so good or the fact that Anatoki had given it to him. He had never eaten a better meal. He ate three chickens without stopping.

"Whoa, my little wolf. I'm happy to have you sleep in my room, but I don't want you sick to your stomach all night. That's enough for now. You don't have to worry about when you'll eat again as long as you're here. There'll always be food when you're hungry," Anatoki said as she gave Dakar a hug. Auatuyi had stiffened as his mistress put her arms around the wolf's neck, for that would normally be dangerous when a wolf was eating. However, Auatuyi soon relaxed, for Dakar only turned his head and gave Anatoki a big lick and put his paw in her lap.

Kattana observed the bond developing between Anatoki and Dakar with a satisfied look. "Okay, I know how tired you must be. You've had a difficult journey, Dakar. There's a lot we each want to know about the other, but it'll keep until tomorrow. Rest is now the best thing for your wound. I've given you the medicine. Let's all go to bed, and we'll talk in the morning," Kattana said as he slowly stood and shuffled down the hallway to his room. "I know you're in good hands with Anatoki."

Dakar's mind was whirling. Everything about this evening was completely foreign and unexpected. His life had been so ordered and predictable. Rahwa was right; his life would definitely never be the same. He was so tired now. He would sort it out later.

"Come on, my dear patient. I've got to get you some soft blankets and put you to bed. Papa's done all he can for you tonight, but I'll give you a big hug and a kiss. That's my medicine."

Dakar had no doubt that Anatoki's medicine was at least as good as her fathers'.

However, he had feelings of guilt while lying in bed. *I wonder where my family is tonight? I'm worried about them. I hope those hunters aren't after them now,* he thought.

CHAPTER 18

Tanya was up at daylight. She was getting very nervous now, for it had been three days since Dakar had left. Torga heard her stirring around outside the small den they were using, and he knew she was thinking about the need to arrange a permanent den for the cubs she was bearing.

"All right, everybody. Let's get started. We've got to find Dakar within a few days, or else we're going to have to start a den for Tanya. We can't wait any longer," Torga gruffed.

`"Torga, do you think we'll find him today?" Tanya asked, as she entered the depression in the hill they were using for a den. "I heard you, and you're right. I can tell it will be only a couple of days before I have to stop and get ready for the cubs. I'm *so* scared for my Dakar," she whined. Torga had to turn away from the soulful look in her soft amber eyes. Her head was down, and her body seemed to sag and shorten.

Torga now knew he couldn't let anything stand in the way of their search. If there were any more obstacles he would deal with them more forcefully, for he wasn't going to let Tanya suffer any more. Tagar and Pika were mouthing each other and rolling around down the hillside; they were chaffing under the strict discipline Torga enforced on the pack during their journey. Torga's eyes narrowed into slits and his tail raised like a flag. He growled deeply and fixed his eyes on the cubs, staring intensely. When they saw his look, they immediately came over to him with their tails between their legs and their heads down. Torga placed his forelegs across the shoulders of Tagar and nipped the cub's neck. He then got off Tagar and looked at Pika with his mouth wide and his teeth bared. He got into a crouch similar to one he would use in a surprise attack and growled deeply at both cubs. They quickly got into a submissive posture lying on their backs with their legs spread out exposing their stomachs to Torga.

"I think you both understand now that no more insubordination will be allowed the rest of this trip. You are under strict pack discipline until I say you are free to play again. I think you know what will happen next time," Torga growled. "We have a difficult and probably dangerous journey ahead of us, and every member of this pack has to be alert to danger and on guard at all times. Our strength lies in the whole of the pack; it's time you understood that and became a responsible member." The sheepish expressions on the cubs showed that he had made his point, at least for the moment.

Torga then paced purposefully down the mountain to the spot where he had last smelled Dakar's scent. He hadn't told Tanya that he could also tell Dakar's injury was getting worse; he picked that up in the scent. No need to tell her until they found Dakar. It might not be as serious as he thought, and then she would be needlessly worried.

"I can tell that Dakar has picked up his pace from here. He seems to know where he's going, but I have no idea why he would want to go someplace this far south of our home. He must be getting some help from someone or something we don't know about. That would explain how he made it through the wolf pack's territory. I don't think he would have taken a chance on going straight through their boundaries otherwise. At least, I hope I taught him better than that," Torga said to Tanya. "Somehow he's being directed this way; his trail and the direct route he's taking would have no other explanation. We'll just have to follow until he gets where he's headed. Then we'll catch up."

Tanya's eyes drooped, and her head dropped a bit. She was not sure when she would see her beloved Dakar again. Torga took a few minutes to rub against her and lick her face and ears. Then, he led the pack down the path by the Flathead River following Dakar's trail.

*   *   *

John Sanders was awakened early in the morning by the sound of banging on his door. He and his group had made it down the mountain and gotten a ride to the town of Elkford. There, a local doctor had made repairs to his arm and Tremaine's leg. His arm was broken, but Tremaine only had ligament damage and could walk fairly well with a brace provided by the doctor.

"Who is it?" Sanders yelled, irritated that he was awakened before daylight.

"It's me, Henry!" Winslow answered. "I thought I'd get you up so we can get an early start. Jacque found out where we can get some guns, and we're ready to go!"

Sanders slowly got out of bed, grabbed his shirt with his one good arm, and put it over his shoulders. As he opened the door, he said, "You've sure changed your schedule. I thought you didn't like to get up until well into the day."

"Look, we've been put through the wringer, and now we want revenge. You wouldn't believe it, but Ben's almost dressed. He's even looking forward to tracking that wolf and hiking all day after him, if necessary. No more planes, though."

Sanders started getting his clothes together. He hadn't yet gotten the hang of dressing with his arm in a cast. "I take it you guys didn't visit any bars last night after I left you."

Winslow's face turned red, and he looked down at the floor for a second. "All right, we've learned our lesson. This is serious business, and you can't mix business and pleasure. We've got it. Let's drop that subject now and get on with the hunt. We won't rest easy until we've gotten that durn wolf."

Sanders smiled. "Fair enough. You don't mention the plane crash, and I won't mention anything about you fellows' conduct the last few days. Deal!"

After breakfast at a diner, they went to a hardware store and obtained three rifles. Sanders couldn't use a rifle, so he bought a pistol, more for protection than as a hunting weapon.

Tunnell turned to Tremaine as they left the store. "I don't know how you persuaded that store owner to open early for us, but it sure does beat waiting around all morning!"

Tremaine smiled, his look almost friendly. "You guys have come a long way in one day. I guess the need for revenge gives a man backbone." He put his arm around Tunnell and gave a slight squeeze to Tunnell's shoulder.

`Winslow grinned. "I know one thing it does, it sure makes a dent in my credit card account. It's a good thing I've got a high credit limit, because we've done a good job of eating into it already, and the day's just getting started."

"Sorry I couldn't find my billfold, Henry," Tunnell apologized. "You know I'll pay you back as soon as we're home."

"No problem. Now, where's that guy you hired to take us back to the trail, Jacque?" Winslow answered.

"Right down the street. He's in that blue Wagoneer. He told me to look for it. It's the only one in town."

Tremaine walked down towards the vehicle, taking a step with his good leg and dragging the one with the brace. "Let's get on the trail, Mon Chers."

Soon after being let off near where the group had descended from the mountain, Tremaine called out, "Over here!"

When the others came over he said, "Look at these tracks! This is a whole pack of wolves! I don't believe in coincidences like this; I think our wolf's family is following him. We could walk around these parts for several years and not find a wolf pack's prints here below the mountains."

Sanders had a huge grin on his face. "My arm feels better already. Okay, fellows, you wanted revenge, now you're going to get it! Let's just follow the pack, and we'll get them and maybe the young one we've been after, too."

*   *   *

The morning light shining through Anatoki's window woke Dakar. He had slept soundly throughout the night. When he awoke, the first thing he did was look up at the bed to see if Anatoki was there. She was the most beautiful being he had ever seen. He didn't know such beauty existed in the world. Rahwa was definitely right. This journey was important to him. He looked over in the corner where Auatuyi was still sleeping. The dog would be a good friend. While Auatuyi was older and domesticated, he had enough of the old instincts in him to realize Dakar's dominant status. He would not challenge Dakar over anything important, and they both certainly agreed on the importance of caring for Anatoki.

I can't believe how comfortable I am here with these humans, Dakar thought. Only a day before, he hadn't believed he would even be able to be in their company. Humans were certainly not as easy to understand as he thought. They were all not the bloodthirsty animals he had thought, but he realized it was difficult to know which were which. The wolf world was much simpler; the patterns and social structure were pretty much universal. You knew the rules, and if you followed them, you had no trouble with your own kind. If there were rules in the human world, they must be very complicated.

Dakar silently stood and noticed immediately that his shoulder felt better. He could put some weight on it, and he could tell it would mend with time. He didn't know how much time he had, for he was worried about his family. *What if the hunters decide to go after them?* he thought. *My place is really helping them, not here safe while they may be in danger.*

Anatoki stirred and her arm moved casually across the bed towards Dakar. As she set her hand down, it was right next to his face. Impulsively, he licked her fingers with a soft, gentle motion.

Anatoki's eyes slowly opened, and she smiled and said, "Oh, good morning, my beautiful wolf. Why don't you come up here in the bed and let me give you a big good morning hug."

Dakar literally flew through the air and landed on Anatoki with a thud.

"Whoops, Dakar! You will have to learn I'm not a wolf. I'm just a little girl. You almost knocked all the air out of me!" Anatoki said with a giggle.

Dakar's eyes fell, and Anatoki could see the bottom lid hang down. Dakar's whole body sagged, and he said, "Oh, No! I didn't *mean* to hurt you! I'm sorry! I won't ever do it again. I have a brother and sister, and I've never played with anyone else, except, of course, Meyote. She's a little grizzly bear cub I met through Rahwa on this trip. I'll be careful with you from now on, you'll see."

"Oh, Dakar, relax!" Anatoki said with a grin. "I was just teasing you. I didn't mean to hurt your feelings. I know you're a wolf. I know you'll have to get used to playing with me. Gosh, you must have already had an exciting life! You played with a grizzly bear, huh? We'll have to have long talks, and you can tell me everything about your life and all the interesting things you've done already."

Dakar noticeably puffed up with pride, and his eyes and ears became alert and erect. "Well, I *have* led an exciting life, I guess. I'd be glad to tell you all about it. I can teach you how to hunt moose and caribou and lots of other things, too."

Anatoki's face radiated with the most perfect smile Dakar had ever seen. She laughed and said, "Well, Dakar, I'm afraid those days are gone for us Indians, unfortunately. I'd love to hear you tell how you do it, though. There's a lake near here, Lake Sherburne. When it gets warmer, we'll go sit by the lake and watch the ducks; you can tell me about your life, and I'll tell you about mine. Would you like that?"

Before he thought, Dakar gushed, "Oh, more than anything in the world!" Dakar thrust his head forward and quickly licked Anatoki's face with small gentle licks until he had covered her whole face.

Anatoki giggled. "I can tell I'm going to have to carry extra handkerchiefs when I'm with you, Dakar!" Dakar just beamed, even though he had no idea what a handkerchief was.

Auatuki looked up from his bed in the corner and said, "I can see I'm not going to get to sleep late while you're here, Dakar. Is there something you have to do this time of morning that can't wait for a decent hour?"

"You've gotten soft living this sheltered life in a house with people to take care of you. We wolves have to get up early to go hunt. We have to take care of ourselves," Dakar answered with a proud look of self-confidence.

"Yeah, well, I can see that you're getting awfully comfortable with this lifestyle; I take it you kinda like my mistress, huh?"

"She is *wonderful*! I didn't know any humans existed like her!"

Anatoki had left the room for a minute, and she came back as Dakar finished talking about her. "Oh, Dakar, you're so charming!" She said, as she put her arms around his neck and gave him a big hug. Dakar collapsed on his back after she let go, and his eyes were glazed and staring into space.

I don't know what's come over me, Dakar thought. *But I've got to get myself together and start worrying about my family. They may need me right now.*

Anatoki got dressed, and they went into the kitchen. Dakar followed right beside her and saw that Kattana was already up and doing something on a counter with food that smelled strange but surprisingly good. The kitchen was rustic but immaculately clean. Dakar noticed for the first time that there were lots of strange-looking objects in the room that made a humming noise. Kattana opened one of them, and Dakar felt a blast of cold air carrying delicious smells from inside the object. The floor of the kitchen was a well-kept but old type of solid material that yielded to his toenails. The cabinets were made of wood and had several layers of wood in some sort of design on their face.

Kattana saw them and said, "Well, good morning, Dakar. How's the shoulder this morning? You seem to be walking on it a little bit today."

"Yes, it's much better. I can tell that whatever you did is really helping. It doesn't feel nearly as hot as it did yesterday, either."

"I was sure it would. We've been using that medicine for hundreds of years. It's served us well. Rahwa is outside and wants to have a word with you. Here, I'll open the door for you." Kattana then opened the wooden door.

Rahwa was standing on the wood picket fence, which enclosed the yard of the house. Dakar immediately noticed that Rahwa's face had a sorrowful expression, and his head was stretched downward, giving him a look of complete sadness.

"Rahwa, what's wrong? You look like something terrible has happened!" Dakar said with alarm. Dakar sat in front of

Rahwa with his ears erect and his sensitive eyes staring at the raven.

"Dakar, the time has come for me to leave. I've done what I came to do. You've learned that all humans aren't bad; that's a good start. You are in good hands, and I'm sure you will learn much from Kattana. It will make you a better wolf and a better pack leader. Also, I hope you will have an opportunity to influence humans' ideas about wolves' true nature. The only hope for your kind is to have humans in powerful positions appreciate your true worth. It didn't happen in time for the Indians, and Kattana can tell you what the results were. I hope that you will learn from the history of the Indians and help make sure it doesn't happen to wolves. That's what I was sent here to do. Although I know you don't have the slightest idea what I'm talking about, you might say I'm sort of a guardian angel for wolves and other worthy animals. I met your father when he was about your age. He's a good wolf, but he wasn't prepared to accept me. His generation is too set in its ways, just like the last generation of humans. The hope for the future lies in wolves like you. One day I hope my trust in your good judgment will be proven to be right."

Dakar looked at Rahwa, cocking his head from side to side as if a different angle would make him understand Rahwa better. He then said, "Rahwa, we're friends now. I don't want you to leave. There's so much I still need to learn from you. Stay here. Please."

"No, Dakar. Kattana knows I have to go. Maybe he can explain it better than I. I also know what you are feeling for Anatoki, but that isn't your destiny. You aren't like Auatuyi, and it would take 5,000 years of evolution for you to be like him. I know you don't understand what that means, but it means it would be impossible for you to live here with Anatoki, no matter how much you care for her. In another time, several generations ago, it might have been possible. The Indians in those days had lives similar to the lives of wolves. It was a better time, but that period is gone forever. You have to live in the present, and you have a responsibility to your kind. You can't neglect it. Maybe someday I'll visit you again. I hope so. Don't let me down, Dakar, I've got a lot of faith in you. Make me proud!" As Rahwa finished talking, his wings began to glow, and he rose higher and higher without moving his wings. "Goodbye, Dakar, my friend." Rahwa smiled, and the area around his face shone with a brilliant yellow halo. As he rose, he winked at Dakar, and a flash of white light made Dakar shut his eyes momentarily. Then, he ascended so quickly Dakar couldn't follow his movement. Before Dakar could say or do anything Rahwa had disappeared into the clouds, a blazing white trail marking his ascension into the sky.

Dakar just stared up at the clouds for several minutes, completely confused. Suddenly, Dakar was aware that Kattana was standing beside him. Kattana had an air of dignity and strength of character about him that reminded Dakar of his father. Kattana radiated the same power, together with the same gentleness. Kattana stood silently beside Dakar with his hand on Dakar's shoulder looking at the clouds.

Finally, Dakar turned, looked up at Kattana, and asked, "Just what is Rahwa? I know he's more than a raven, but I don't understand what he really is."

"It is difficult to explain. There is a Rahwa that may come to all of us, but we usually aren't ready to accept him. Probably when you saved the lives of your family, Rahwa came to you because you proved yourself worthy. You took a chance on sacrificing yourself for a noble purpose. That used to happen much more than it does now, and people were visited by their good spirits and aided because they were deemed worthy. A good spirit can take many forms, but often the animal spirit is a raven. We Blackfeet have always considered the raven to be very wise. He knows more than any of the birds. We have found that he always tells the truth, so we watch his actions very carefully. In the old days, when we were hunting buffalo, if we saw ravens playing together on a ridge, we took our course in that direction. If we were on a war party and we saw ravens with their heads close together on our trail, we set up an ambush because the ravens were warning us that an enemy was approaching. Your good spirit probably chose Rahwa because you wolves live a life very much like we used to live. Rahwa is a good friend of ours, and he is a good spirit for many animals."

Dakar angled his head from side to side. He was trying to understand so much that was new to him. "Rahwa also said wolves lived a lot like you used to live. I guess that's why you're one of the few humans that can talk to us. Why did you change the way you lived?"

"We were forced to change by the people that came from another land far away. They had all those weapons that are now used to kill animals. They used them to kill us too in those days. They said we had to learn to live like they did or they would kill us. They did kill most of us. It is from among those people that you have the enemies you must fear, not us."

"Did you Indians ever kill wolves, too?" Dakar asked.

"Come inside, Dakar. I'll tell you a story that has been told many times around the campfires of our people. It answers your question, but it also may tell you something about why you're here. I want Anatoki to hear it too; she's never heard this story. I think it may answer why you and she were so immediately drawn to one another."

CHAPTER 19

Dakar ran into the house ahead of Kattana. He had momentarily forgotten about his questions concerning Rahwa. Anything that could help explain why he was so drawn to Anatoki was vitally important to him.

Dakar found Anatoki at the table in a small alcove off the kitchen eating breakfast. She looked up in surprise as Dakar bounded into the room, and Dakar said, "Quick, Anatoki! Come in the other room. Your father's going to tell a story that concerns you and me!"

Anatoki smiled at Dakar's excitement. "Dakar, relax. We've got lots of time to listen to father's stories. You'll hear them endlessly. Oh, all right, let's go in the living room and get comfortable. I get the feeling this will be a long one."

Anatoki got up and Dakar took up a position right next to her as they walked down a short hallway into the living room. He was comfortable in this room. It had wood walls, which reminded him of the forests of his home territory. There was old but well-preserved furniture, mostly overstuffed. The wood floor was mostly covered with a rug, hand-woven with intricate Indian designs. On the walls were mementos of a long-gone era: an Indian headdress, a shield, a medicine bundle rolled up in beaver skin, and old photos of Indians in their native costume. Anatoki sat down on the large stuffed sofa and drew her legs up under her. Dakar jumped upon the sofa next to her and put his head in her lap. She placed her hand on top of his head and casually rubbed his ears. He had never had anything feel so good. He was as comfortable as if he were in his den next to his mother.

"Okay, children. I'm going to tell you a story that has been told around the campfires of many Blackfoot camps," Kattana began. "Many years ago, a large party of Crow Indians attacked the Blackfoot while we were moving camp. They raided the center of the line where the women and children were. They carried away some women prisoners; one of which was named Itsa-pich-kaupe (Sits-by-the-door). She was carried back to the Crow camp. A Crow woman there felt sorry for her and helped her escape. She ran out of food and her feet were bruised and bleeding. A wolf that had been watching her crept nearer and nearer until he lay at her feet. She prayed to the wolf to help her. The wolf soon left, but he came back later dragging a buffalo calf he had just killed. After eating some of the meat, she felt stronger and tried to walk, but she was too weak. The wolf stood beside her and let her place her hand on his back for support. He kept her supplied with food every day until he brought her back to camp. She asked her family to be kind to the wolf and feed him. However, our camp dogs drove the wolf out of camp and wouldn't let him return. He would sit every evening at the summit of a high butte gazing at the lodge where Itsa-pich-kaupe lay. Her relatives continued to feed him until he finally disappeared. To this day, the Blackfoot never shoot at a wolf, believing them to be good medicine. We have a saying, 'The gun that shoots a wolf will never again shoot straight'. Anatoki, Itsa-pich-kaupe was your great-grandmother!"

Anatoki was astonished. She had never heard this story before. Tears came to her eyes, and she bent down and hugged Dakar's neck tightly, the tears making spots on his grey fur. Dakar lifted his head and looked softly at Anatoki. Then, he gently licked her eyes with small, comforting licks.

I wonder if I could possibly be related to the wolf in the story? Dakar thought. *I would have done that for Anatoki. I would do it now.*

Kattana continued, "At one time, all animals and men could understand one another. While we still talk to the animals, most seldom reply, except in dreams. Whenever we were in danger in the old days, we would pray to animals and they often would help us. I believe that is why Rahwa brought you here, Dakar. First, my family and we Blackfeet particularly owe you wolves a great debt. Secondly, I think Rahwa recognized that you will one day be a leader of wolves, and he wanted you to learn from the experiences of us Indians. Maybe somehow you can learn to exist with the white faces. One thing is for sure, Anatoki has the chance to make up for the fact that her great-grandmother never got the chance to thank that wolf. Also, I don't think Auatuyi here is going to run you out of our camp."

Auatuyi, who had been lying right beside Kattana's rocking chair, looked up with an irritated expression and said, "Don't blame me for what those dogs did! Dakar and I are friends!" Auatuyi slowly got up, stretched, and then went over to Dakar and gave him a lick on his nose.

"Don't worry, my friend," Dakar said. "We wolves wouldn't hold a grudge against anyone for something they didn't do."

Anatoki smiled. Then her face took on a very thoughtful expression. "Papa, do you think Dakar could be descended from the wolf in the story? Wouldn't that be wonderful! We'll have the chance to make it all up to you, Dakar." Dakar rolled over on his back on the sofa, and Anatoki slowly scratched his belly with her long fingernails. Dakar felt she had already gone a long way towards making up any injustice to his forefathers.

Kattana's eyes twinkled, and he smiled as he said, "I think you're going to spoil that wolf so much that no one is going to be able to be around him! Dakar, I know you need to get back to your family. But, at least until you're well, stay here. Maybe I can teach you some things about humans that will help you and your pack."

"I feel guilty being this safe and comfortable and not knowing the fate of my family," Dakar answered. "Those humans that tried to kill my family may still be trying, and I've got to help. It would be wonderful to stay here for days and learn more from you both, but as soon as I possibly can, I've got to start going back to my home territory."

"I've got an idea!" Anatoki exclaimed. "Papa's got a tipi outside that was built just like they built them in the old days. Well, almost the same. They used to use buffalo skins, and he used canvas. Why don't you, Auatuyi, and I stay out there tonight, Dakar? Then, it'll be just like the story Papa told, only this time you'll get to stay in the lodge with me. We can play like we're the people in the story, and you'll get to be with the girl this time. Let's have fun for whatever time you can spend with us!"

Dakar smiled and said, "That sounds like a great idea. I'm not used to staying in a house, and if we're outside I can still hear the noises of the night."

"Come, I'll show it to you," Anatoki replied.

They went out the back door and through a gate in the wooden fence. About 100 feet beyond the fence in a grove of pine stood the tipi. It was about twenty-four feet in diameter, and twenty-two poles were used for the supporting framework. They were around thirty feet long. There were two "ear-poles" used to allow smoke to escape. All the poles were made of pine. The opening was made by taking the two flap ends and pinning them above the door opening with seven slender sticks. Inside there was a fireplace made of stone right in the center. Around the fireplace, in a adjustment to civilization, there were several bed rolls.

Dakar stepped carefully inside the opening, and he then said, "You know, you Indians did live a lot like we wolves. This isn't a lot different from our den, except we don't have a place where fire is kept. Did you have more than one of these?"

"Not usually. We would take the tipi down when we moved and set it up again at the new camp."

"Well, that's not a lot different from us. We sometimes have several dens, but of course we can't move them. We just build another one someplace else. We sometimes use more than one at a time, though."

Auatuyi, who had been listening to the conversation, raised his head and asked, "Dakar, do you think you could teach me to build a den? I'd like to learn something about the way my ancestors lived, too."

Anatoki reached over and gave Auatuyi a hug and said, "Do you feel left out, my friend? I guess Dakar is making us all think about how we got to where we are. And, where we're going, too."

Dakar felt at home in the tipi with Anatoki and Auatuyi. The tipi gave him the same secure feeling he had in his den, and Anatoki, Kattana, and Auatuyi were beginning to feel like family. His wound was feeling better, too, and he lay awake thinking about how much he would miss his new friends when he had to leave.

*   *   *

Torga led Tanya and the pack down the trail, looking in every direction. He constantly sniffed the air for any strange smells, and he would make the pack hold still every so often while he listened with his sensitive ears for any unusual sounds. He knew that one mistake could be fatal. He had no escape paths located, and he didn't know the terrain.

Fortunately, it was still cold, and there was lots of snow scattered about. Torga knew that the humans generally didn't venture far back into the high country when there was still snow. Soon, Torga found the spot where Dakar had taken the trail over the mountains. Torga had never crossed the high mountains to the east, and he was nervous about taking the pack, not to mention his beloved Tanya, over something so menacing without knowing what they might encounter.

"It looks like Dakar took this path up the high mountains. Are you sure you're up to making a climb like this?" Torga asked Tanya. "We don't know what we'll run into, and we don't know anything about what's on the other side."

Tanya shook her head and curled her lip. "When will you learn that I'm not a fragile cub? Even with the babies, I can take care of myself very well. Let's go. We're just wasting time." To punctuate the point, Tanya took off up the trail knowing that, while it was technically a breach of pack etiquette, Torga would understand that she wasn't challenging his leadership.

Torga growled softly and turned to Tagar. "Remember, Son, even if you become a pack leader some day, you'll never be able to control your mate. She might let you think you're in control, but she'll end up doing pretty much what she wants."

Tagar listened to his father intently. It was apparent that Tagar was pleased that his father chose to give him advice of any kind. He wagged his tail and licked his father's mouth to show his appreciation.

Torga caught up to Tanya and then took over the lead. He couldn't afford to let her have the lead for too long; others in the pack might get the wrong idea. He actually felt safer once he got higher up into the mountains, especially after he got to a place the humans called Boulder Pass. It was around 7,000 feet high and covered with deep snow. His experience had taught him that humans were unlikely to be anywhere the snow was this deep, unless they came in that metal bird. It was now close to noon, and Torga didn't know how high these mountains were, or if Dakar was still anywhere in them. He stopped the pack for a rest and went over to an outcropping rock above the pack to think. From this vantage point, he could see in all directions and make sure the pack was safe. He noticed how beautiful this area was, with lakes to the south and trees of all descriptions just below them. He had stopped several hundred feet above treeline so that his view would not be hindered while he thought.

Finally, he came back to the pack and strolled over to Tanya. "I don't know what Dakar is up to, or why he chose this path. However, we are safer in these mountains than anywhere else we've been since we left our territory. We can find plenty of places in here for a den. Let's just keep on his trail, and if the time comes that you think you're ready to build a den, just let me know." Torga watched Tanya's reaction carefully, for he knew that she wouldn't tell him if she was getting tired or scared. She was too good a mother and Dakar was too important to her.

Tanya's reaction was immediate. She wagged her tail, smiled happily, and got into a crouch so that her head was well below Torga's. She then turned so that her side was to his head and turned her head sideways to lick his face. "Thank you. I promise I won't do anything to endanger the cubs I'm carrying. I'll feel *so* much better when we find Dakar. It'll be much better for the new cubs. You'll see."

"Okay. If you're ready, let's get started. I'd like to go as far as we can before we have to den up for the night. I think that the further we get into these mountains, the safer we'll be. I haven't smelled any fresh signs of humans for several hours."

Torga led them forward on the trail. After about a half hour, they crossed another pass and then started going downhill. Before long, they were at the lake the humans called Waterton, and the scenery around the lake was so beautiful Torga stopped the pack so that they could enjoy the view. While most of the lake was still frozen, there were places where the ice had melted. In those locations, birds of all descriptions were congregated. There were several varieties of swans and many types of ducks. He noticed that there were several heron at each opening in the ice patiently waiting until an unwary fish got too close to the surface. He watched as a heron thrust his beak down into the water and surfaced with a fish that looked too large for the bird's narrow throat. He couldn't believe it when he saw the bird swallow the fish whole, and he watched as the throat stretched while the fish went down its length.

There were dense forests of spruce, fir, and lodgepole pine all around the lake. He could see the pack staying at a spot like this for quite a while, if only they had Dakar with them.

Torga walked a little farther along the trail, then stopped suddenly. "Tanya, I get a very strong scent of Dakar here. He must have stopped, just like we're doing. There's something else, though. It's a smell I remember from when I was a cub; I haven't smelled it since. I somehow know it's a good sign, though. Someone or something is with Dakar, and I sense that it's looking out for him. I'm sure it has something to do with why he's taking this path. I think Dakar will be all right."

Tanya looked at Torga inquisitively. "I don't understand. Who could be with Dakar? How do you know he's going to be okay?"

"The scent brings back a memory from my childhood; I can't quite get a paw on it, but I *know* it's something good. I remember it was something that was much more important than it appeared to be, but that's all I remember."

211

"Torga, are you all right? I don't understand what you're trying to tell me." Tanya cocked her head from side to side, obviously very confused.

"Don't worry. It's one of those things you can't explain, like how our cubs just appear one day, or how we just *know* when there's a herd of moose somewhere close." Torga started down the trail, knowing he wouldn't be able to explain what he didn't really understand himself.

He had been traveling down the trail for about an hour, past some majestic waterfalls, when he motioned for the pack to stop. "We've been going downhill since before the sun was high. I think we're going to be past these mountains before too long. I don't want to be away from the safety of mountains after dark. We don't know what's on the other side. I see a lot of lakes just south of us, and where there are lakes this time of year there's game. We'll stop here and find a place to den up. Then Mutar, Maya, and I will go find dinner." The pack all got excited at the thought of dinner, for they had been walking for quite a while without eating.

Torga had stopped at a bend in the trail, and he took Tanya through some spruce trees just south of the trail looking for a den. As they exited the cover of a particularly dense clump of trees, Tanya involuntarily gasped. "Look, Torga!"

There, in front of them, was a cluster of five lakes with a waterfall right next to them.

"This is the most lovely spot I've ever seen in my life! Do you think we could come back here after we find Dakar? This would be such a perfect place to raise our cubs!" Tanya exclaimed.

Torga didn't say anything for a while. He knew that Dakar could be almost anywhere. Here, in unknown country, he didn't have any idea what lay in store for them. He decided that it wasn't necessary to worry Tanya needlessly. "I suppose so. Let's see what happens tomorrow. Right now, I see a promising spot behind that waterfall. Let's check on it."

Torga found that there was an opening in the rock right behind the waterfall. It was hidden until he was almost at the falls, and from that spot Torga could see hundreds of feet in all directions. *This will be perfect for a den,* he thought. He left Tanya to decide how she wanted to organize the den, and he went back for the pack.

When he returned, Tanya had prepared some bedding out of dead leaves and pine needles she had gotten from under the

213

Louis Dorfman

snow around the waterfall. "I know you don't want to make a decision now, but if everything works out all right, I really want to have the cubs here. This place is even more lovely than the territory we had up north."

"We'll see. I'll have Surle and Halwa stay here with you and the cubs. They can help you gather more bedding, in case we *do* stay."

Torga, Mutar, and Maya returned with some grouse and several hares for dinner. The hungry wolves ate quickly, having expended a great deal of energy that day on the trip.

As soon as they had finished eating, Torga gathered the pack. "I didn't pick up any scent of other wolves anywhere around here, so this territory is open. We may think about making this our new territory after we find Dakar."

The pack obviously shared Tanya's love for this area. The wolves started jumping up and down, and they climbed all over each other in play, nipping each other's heels. Tagar and Pika joined in the play, but they were restrained, remembering their father's words to them. Torga left Tanya and the pack to make one last search of the area before they settled down for the night.

*   *   *

John Sanders was tired. He knew his clients must be completely exhausted. They had followed the wolf pack's footprints almost across Glacier National Park. He only now realized how much these two clients wanted revenge. He wouldn't have thought they had it in them to make the grueling trip they had made. Now, however, they were about to reap the harvest of their efforts.

"Jacque," Sanders said, "you're sure you saw where those wolves went into the rock?"

"Oui, you know if I say I saw it, I saw it. They found an opening behind a waterfall just over the ridge. It's about thirty feet below that rock outcrop we're looking at. All we have to do is wait until morning."

Winslow smiled with more feeling than he had felt in three days. "Well, Ben, it looks like we're going to get more than just one trophy apiece. We're going to be the envy of all our friends."

"Yeah, Henry, but we will have earned it!" Tunnell answered. "My feet feel like one huge blister. And my legs feel like two pieces of spaghetti. I don't think I'll get over this day for a long time."

Sanders smiled at the exchange. The two clients were actually feeling better than they had since he met them. Too bad they couldn't devote all that energy and emotion into something meaningful. He had to admit that now that they were about to end the existence of the wolf pack, he regretted it. The wolves were worthy adversaries, but in the final analysis they wouldn't have a chance against three rifles and a pistol. *I know I'll have an empty feeling when it's over tomorrow,* he thought. *It won't take five minutes, and then I'll wonder if killing a group of animals that didn't do anything to bother us was worth it. Oh, well. I'll be richer for it.* "What should the plan be, Jacque?" Sanders asked.

"We'll form a line along the hillside by the path of the waterfall. In the morning they'll have to come out of the den for water, if nothing else. We'll wait till they're all out of the den, then I'll say when to shoot. We'll all shoot at once. Those of us closest to the waterfall will take out the wolves to the left and so on down the line," Tremaine said as calmly as if he was explaining how to go to the post office.

Tunnell pulled his down-filled jacket closely around his body and put on his gloves. "Boy, I'm sure glad we found that store just before the mountains and got these clothes. It's going to be a long and cold night."

"Yeah, but just think how much fun and satisfaction we'll have in the morning!" Winslow offered, his face beginning to get the glazed, feverish expression of a fanatic.

CHAPTER 20

Torga didn't think there was any danger to the pack in this remote territory, but he learned long ago not to ever take safety for granted. He always made a last pass around the immediately adjacent terrain before denning up for the night. As tired as he was, he wasn't going to change his policy here. He had started on the eastern side of the waterfall, and he was half-way around the circle he was making when he suddenly picked up the hated odor of humans. *No!* he thought. *Just when I thought we had made it safely across this strange land. And the smell is familiar. It's those humans that tried to kill Tanya and the cubs!*

Now, he changed his pace to a stalk. He crept closer to the smell, moving one tentative step at a time. He made sure he didn't make a sound or make a single branch move on the bushes beside him. As he inched closer he could hear the voices of the dreaded hunters, and he only chanced getting close enough to see how many there were. *It's the same four humans that came in the metal bird,* he thought. *They have those metal sticks that make the loud noise and kill us.*

Torga crawled backward and retraced his steps to the den. He knew those humans were after his pack, and he had to assume they knew where the pack was. *I don't know how I'm going to get my loved ones out of the den and to safety, with the humans so close,* he thought.

As soon as he arrived back at the den he quickly gathered the pack. "We've got real trouble! Those humans that tried to kill Tanya and the cubs are just above us. They must have followed our trail. There's no other way out of here except by the waterfall, and they are probably watching it. We can make a run for it, but I'm afraid they'll kill some of us." Torga stole a look at Tanya and was sorry that he had. She was obviously horrified. Her eyes were wide and unfocused. She was shaking like she was standing in the middle of a winter storm.

Finally she collected herself enough to ask, "Isn't there anything we can do? There must be some solution. We can't have come all this way just to end up like this!"

"There is one possibility," Torga answered. "Dakar's scent is strong. He passed this way not long ago. We can howl for him and tell him what's happened. If he can hear us, maybe he can do something. Maybe he can at least make a diversion, like he did last time, so we can get out of this den safely."

"But last time Dakar was healthy!" Tanya implored. "We know he's injured now. He wouldn't be as strong or as fast!"

"I know that," Torga said sadly. "I have to think of the good of the pack, not to mention the cubs still inside you." Tanya looked down at the ground and whimpered. Her tail was whirling like a windmill, and the hair on her back was standing out from her body. Torga looked away, unable to face his beloved Tanya. *There are times when I wish I weren't pack leader,* he thought.

Torga got the pack together at the entrance to the den. They howled their message as loudly and as long as they could. The solid stone walls behind them served to magnify their sounds in the clear night air.

*   *   *

Dakar was nearly asleep when he heard a familiar sound; he couldn't decide at first whether he was dreaming or not. He had dreamed about his pack many times since he'd left them. Initially he thought this was just another dream. Then he sat up in the tipi, and his ears perked up. Yes! It *was* his pack! He could recognize the voice of each member. There! That was his beloved mother. He couldn't believe that they had followed him all the way here. He knew his mother was about to have some more cubs. He could tell they were calling for him. *Wait!* he thought. *They're in danger! Those horrible humans have followed them and have them surrounded! I must go to them now!*

Anatoki lifted her head when Dakar jumped out of her arm. She had been sleeping with one of her arms around his shoulder. "What's wrong, Dakar? You look like you hear something. Is there someone outside?"

Dakar realized that humans couldn't hear nearly as well as wolves. She didn't hear the sounds of his pack. "I hear my family calling. They must have followed me. They're in terrible danger! Those humans that wounded me have them surrounded up in the mountains. I must go to them. Now!"

"Oh, Dakar!" Anatoki said sadly. "I'm *so* sorry! But your shoulder! You have barely begun to heal. The infection is still there!"

"It doesn't matter! It's my family and they're in danger! I've got to leave right now!" Dakar got up and started trying to open the tipi without tearing the canvas.

Auatuyi, who had awakened as soon as Dakar stirred, said, "Let me to go with you. I can help. I may not be as strong as a wolf, but I can still give a good account of myself!"

"No, my friend. This is my responsibility. I handled these humans once, and I can do it again," Dakar said with a look of determination.

"Let's at least talk to Papa. He may have some way of helping. It won't take but a minute!" Anatoki pleaded.

Dakar thought about it. "All right. I can use some help, if he has any ideas. But I don't want to take very long to talk about it. Besides," Dakar said haltingly, "I want to say goodbye. I might not be able to come back. He has been good and kind to me. I owe him at least that."

"Dakar!" Anatoki cried. "Nothing is going to happen to you. I won't let it!" Tears flowed from her eyes, and she threw her arms around Dakar, squeezing him tightly. "I love you, Dakar."

"I love you too."

Anatoki let Dakar go and opened the flaps on the tipi. "Come on. We'll get Papa up. He'll have some good ideas, I bet."

As Dakar entered the kitchen, he was surprised to find that Kattana was sitting in his chair by the breakfast table. He had on a brown robe that was hanging loosely, and he was looking at a black leather-bound book.

Kattana looked up as Dakar, Anatoki, and Auatuyi came in. "Come on in. I was just looking up some phone numbers of friends that might help us."

Dakar cocked his head, trying to make sense of what Kattana said. "I don't understand. Why are you up? You were going to sleep when we left. I've heard from my family. They're…"

Kattana held up his hand. "Don't waste time telling me what I already know. I heard them. I know all about their problem. I'm trying to get help right now."

"I don't understand…"

"We have what are called telephones. They let us speak to our friends, no matter where they are, as long as they have one too. I'm going to call ten of my friends that still live and believe in the 'old' ways. We're going up there with you, Dakar. Those hunters won't do anything till morning. They're going to wait until the pack comes out for food or water. No sense going up there at night, making a lot of noise and warning the hunters that we're coming. We'll go at first light."

"You mean you'd do this for me? Really?"

"Dakar, you're very important to me and to our people. Knowing that creatures like you still live, wild and free, give us

223

hope that the earth hasn't lost all of its natural, uncivilized creations. We need to know you're still out there. Also, our people still owe you a debt. We never rest easy until we repay a debt."

Dakar lifted himself onto the chair next to Kattana and licked Kattana all over his face. "I'll never forget you for helping me at a time like this. Do you really think they'll be okay till morning?"

Kattana put his hand on Dakar's neck, smiled at Dakar, and affectionately rubbed the hair on Dakar's shoulder. "Why don't you step outside and howl back to them? Tell them to stay put, that you'll be there first thing in the morning, and that you're bringing help? Don't tell them what kind of help, though. No sense muddying things up. Just tell them, no matter what, not to leave the den they're in till they hear from you tomorrow."

Dakar pranced outside, his head held high and his tail standing straight up. As soon as he was away from the house, he let out a series of soulful howls that brought chills to the neck of Kattana and Anatoki. The hair on Auatuyi's back stood up. Tears of happiness streamed down Anatoki's face, and she impulsively stepped over to her father, put her arms around his neck, and hugged him tightly. "Thank you, Papa."

Kattana's face turned red, and he looked down. As Dakar stepped back in the house, he was surprised to see several drops of tears falling from Kattana's cheeks.

"All right, you two. I've got work to do," Kattana gruffed. "You two try to get a little rest. We've got a hard day tomorrow. Anatoki, put a bit more medicine on Dakar's shoulder."

CHAPTER 21

Torga and Tanya stood statute-still and listened to the beautiful sounds of their son's voice. They hadn't known if they would ever again hear him. *Now,* Torga thought, *Dakar is again trying to save his family, including his father. What a fine young man!*

Tanya looked at Torga. Light was again in her eyes, and her face loosened from the tight strain she had been feeling for days. "What does he mean, he'll bring help? I can't believe he made friends with some other wolves in just this period of time!"

Torga smiled at Tanya. He was beginning to feel there was hope for the first time in hours. "We won't know until morning. There is something going on that we don't understand. It's that strange force that I feel is with Dakar. He won't be the same cub we last saw. I'm sure of that."

"What do you mean?" Tanya looked curiously at Torga.

"We'll find out tomorrow. I think whatever changes we see, we'll like. He made it this far, and now he's planning to help us again."

Torga turned to the pack, which were all anxiously awaiting some direction from their leader. "Right now, the best thing you can do is rest up from your day's journey. We may have to fight for our lives tomorrow. Be ready!"

*   *   *

Before daylight Indians began arriving at Kattana's house in groups of one or twos. Kattana brought all his friends into the living room, where they sat on the floor, their legs crossed in front of them. As soon as they were all assembled Kattana called Anatoki, and she, Dakar, and Auatuyi came out of her room. There were sighs of appreciation at the beauty and majesty of the wolf in front of them.

Despite his nervousness, Dakar knew he had to act like a leader if he wanted this group of humans to believe he was worth following. "Kattana has told me about your story concerning my ancestor. I've learned from Kattana how much your background and history is like my own. Kattana tells me you are willing to help us and save my family from those other humans. On behalf of my family, I welcome you into our pack!"

Kattana smiled at Dakar, his eyes were twinkling and the creases of his eyes were also smiling. He slowly nodded to

Dakar with a satisfied look. The ten Indians also nodded and talked among themselves, happy to learn that they really *could* still understand the words of wolves.

Anatoki's face beamed, and she bent down and gave Dakar a big hug.

Auatuyi stepped up beside Dakar, looked over at him, and said, "I'm going, too. Don't try to stop me. I'll be quiet as a wolf. Give me this one chance to live like my ancestors!" He gave Dakar a lick on the cheek.

Dakar assumed the posture of a wolf leader. He stood tall and erect, his tail straight up and his ears alert and forward. He turned to Auatuyi. "Just stay right beside me and do what I do. That's the way I learned." He then strode out the door.

Kattana got up. "It's time, men. Remember your skills at silent walking. We'll follow Dakar." The group silently got up, gathered their rifles from the kitchen, and walked out behind Kattana and Anatoki.

After they got several miles up the mountain, Dakar stopped. The sun was just peaking over the horizon. He turned to Kattana and Anatoki. "I'll tell my family we're coming. Maybe they can tell me exactly where they are." Dakar now had the appearance of a wild wolf: every muscle twitching, his ears turning at the slightest sound, and his eyes darting in all directions.

Kattana nodded with appreciation. "I think that's a good idea. If the hunters hear you, they'll just think they may be lucky enough to get another wolf. They're probably anxious to get you, anyway. It'll keep them diverted. When your family answers, they'll think you're headed right for the pack. What we'll do is go around them and come in from behind."

With only a quick look at Anatoki and a smile in return from her, Dakar put his head back and sang in his loudest voice. In the stillness of the dawn the sound reverberated through the peaks of the mountains, sending chills down the backs of the Indians. Soon, the sounds of the pack answered Dakar. The group of Indians looked at each other and smiled, their faces showed the happiness they felt to be a part of something that was so much a part of their heritage. They said nothing, keeping the discipline they had been taught since little boys.

Dakar turned to Kattana. "Do you know a place where you can see five lakes? They are in a den behind a waterfall just below the spot."

Kattana clenched his fist with a satisfied look. "I know *exactly* where that is. I used to play in that cave when I was your age. If you don't mind, Dakar, let me lead now. I know just where those hunters will set up their ambush."

Kattana stepped back and whispered instructions to his friends. Then, he came up beside Dakar. "We're only about thirty minutes from the den. Not long enough after daylight for the hunters to get curious. I've told my friends what to do: when we get close, we'll coordinate so that two Indians sneak up behind each hunter at the same time. I'll position two Indians on the other side of the falls to shoot if it's necessary to save your family. If any escape, you, me, and Auatuyi can handle them."

Dakar nodded. Auatuyi sat down beside Dakar, his mouth curled in a huge smile and his tongue panting with excitement.

"Where's Anatoki going to be?" Dakar asked with concern.

"She's going to be behind me," Kattana answered, looking at Anatoki. "If you're where you're in any danger, it'll just divert Dakar's and my attention from what we need to be doing."

Anatoki nodded without argument.

The Indians crept up silently through the brush, excited to be doing what their ancestors had done for many generations. Dakar marveled at the ease with which creatures the size of humans could melt into the forest background, almost unseen. Dakar decided that they knew what they were doing; he could even imagine them sneaking up on a herd of caribou undetected. Soon, they had circled around the waterfall. Dakar knew where it was by the sound of the rushing water.

Suddenly, Kattana held up his hand for the group to stop. Then, he looked at two of his friends, raised two fingers, then pointed down the hill. He did the same with the next two, but pointed somewhat higher on the hill. He did the same in succession twice more. Then he motioned to Dakar, and they took up positions just beside the waterfall but in the bushes so that Dakar couldn't actually see the water. He knew it was just beyond their position, however.

Dakar snaked through the bushes, one small step at a time, until he could see the waterfall. He looked cautiously downhill and could easily pick out the four hunters sitting behind bushes in a row. Then Dakar slowly turned his head towards the waterfall. He could see the den behind. He thought he could just pick out the image of his majestic father standing at the den entrance. *I'm so lucky*, he thought. *I've got the most wonderful family in the world, and now I've got some great friends, too. How quickly life changes!*

Suddenly, the quiet morning air was pierced by the loud, authoritarian voice of Kattana. "You are surrounded. Don't move so much as an eyelash. We don't want to harm you, but we will if necessary. Put your guns down slowly. You are being observed. Hesitation will get you hurt!"

Dakar quickly glanced at the hunters. He saw their heads turning at the sound of the voice, looking in all directions. They looked at each other, then Dakar saw the tall, redheaded one that shot at his family shrug his shoulders and put down a small metal object he held in his hand. The others then put down their long metal sticks. Dakar could see why. Each of the hunters had two long metal sticks pointed at their backs, poking them until the hunters put the sticks down.

Dakar looked back at the den. He could see the confused activity at the entrance. His father, Torga, was shuffling from side to side, not knowing what to do.

Dakar couldn't hold himself back any longer. With a quick spurt, he bounded out of the bushes toward the den, shouting, "Father, Mother, don't be scared! *These* humans are friends!"

In seconds, Dakar was at the den entrance. Pack protocol and dignity were temporarily suspended. Torga and Tanya rushed to Dakar's sides, with one of the parents on each side. They started licking and rubbing their bodies against him, hardly believing it could really be him.

Finally, Dakar stopped licking long enough to say, "These humans are called Indians, and they are our friends. They saved your lives, and they helped save mine. I've told them they are members of our pack; I hope that's all right."

Torga stopped long enough to listen to Dakar. "I trust your judgment, son. Saving your family twice is good enough for me. From now on, you'll stand beside me!" Just at that moment Tagar and Pika came over, lowered their heads below Dakar in approved submissive position, then showered their brother with licks and whines.

"Come, Father, Mother. Meet our new friends. There's one I particularly like!" Tanya and Torga looked at each other and smiled as they saw Dakar turn his head with embarrassment as he mentioned the human he liked.

The pack followed Dakar out of the den: Torga, Tanya, then the others. At first they stepped carefully, watching in all directions and sniffing the air. Dakar took them up the slope of the hill to the spot above the waterfall where they could see the lakes. There the Indians had assembled with the hunters in front of them, the hunters' hands tied behind them.

As the wolves paced up the trail, Tremaine turned to Sanders and said, "I've seen many things in the mountains and forests. I've never seen nothing like this! How did that little scrawny wolf get these Indians to help him?"

Sanders glumly shook his head, then turned to Kattana. "Tell me, Chief. How *did* that wolf communicate with you and get you to help him?"

Kattana smiled wisely. "You wouldn't believe me if I told you."

Anatoki rushed forward to greet Dakar, followed closely by Auatuyi. As Anatoki threw her arms around Dakar's neck, Torga crouched down and started growling softly.

"Father!" Dakar shouted. "This is my special friend, Anatoki. Don't be worried!"

Tanya looked at Dakar carefully, then turned to Torga. "I think our son is growing up fast. He's got that look I saw in you when we first met."

Tanya then turned to Dakar. "We've got so much to talk about. Do you think it would be safe to keep our den here while I have the cubs? You've been in this territory for a while."

Kattana interrupted. "I can assure you that you'll be safe. You have the word of the Blackfoot Indians. We'll be looking after you and your pack—our pack!" Torga and Tanya looked at each other, each having trouble believing that the Indian could understand them, and that they could understand him.

"We have many things to learn here," Torga said.

Kattana answered. "We have lots of time to teach you what you want to learn. I think Anatoki will be spending plenty of time with your pack, also." Kattana smiled at the sight of Anatoki sitting on the ground with Dakar lying beside her, his head on Anatoki's lap.

Just then, Anatoki looked up behind Kattana. "Papa. Dakar. Look up in that tree!" Anatoki pointed to a tree behind the Indians.

There, twenty feet off the ground on a branch, sat a huge raven.

As Dakar looked at the raven, the raven winked and a bright white light pierced the air. Then, the raven rose off the branch without moving a wing, hovered over Anatoki and Dakar and looked down with a smile on his face. Suddenly a yellow halo of light surrounded him, and he lifted a wing, waved at Dakar, and soared into the sky at such speed no one could actually follow his progress. Only a white trail of light marked his ascent to the clouds.

ABOUT THE AUTHOR

Louis Dorfman has raised and trained many types of exotic animals, including timber wolves. He currently lives in Texas with seventeen animals as his houseguests. He is an Animal Behaviorist and also spends three days a week working with large cats at the International Exotic Feline Sanctuary, home to 68 tigers, lions, cougars, and leopards, where he rehabilitates cats that have been mistreated in order to improve their quality of life. In addition to being a writer, he is a businessman and an attorney. He has appeared on over 50 television shows and over 100 radio shows as an expert on wild predators.

Printed in the United States
1073300005B/122